THE PUPPETEER'S WAYANG

A selection of modern Malaysian poetry

edited and introduced by
Muhammad Haji Salleh

A co-publication project
In Print
and
Dewan Bahasa dan Pustaka Malaysia

1992

British Library Cataloguing in Publication Data: A catalogue record for this book is available from the British Library.

ISBN 1 873 047 11 8

Cover design by Russell Townsend
Typeset by MC Typeset Ltd
Printed by Athenaeum Press

The cover is based on a photograph of a Wayang Kulit puppet, used by permission of Heather Swabey.

First published in 1992 in cooperation with Dewan Bahasa dan Pustaka Malaysia by
In Print Publishing Ltd, 9 Beaufort Terrace, Brighton BN2 2SU, UK.
Tel: (0273) 682836. Fax: (0273) 620958

CONTENTS

Preface vii
Introduction ix

POETRY

A. Ghafar Ibrahim
Age 1
House 28 2
Five Minutes to Now 3
Old Man 5
My Lord Moon Kite 5
Crows 6

A. Samad Said
Wild in the Fire 7
Touch-Me-Nots 9
On the Bunds 9
Anxiety 10
Leaving 11
Under the Twinkling Stars 12
Thank You 13

A. Wahab Ali
Existence 14
The Fallen Image 15
Hello Death 15
Whispers in Kuala Terengganu 16
The Mountain Breaker 17

Baha Zain
A 'Modern Movement' Collage 18
Plea of the Asian Woman 19
Toilet Paper City 20
Woman 21
A Child's Sketch 22
Postponing Truth 23
Those Pills from the Family Planning Clinic 24
Some Notes from the Past 25

Dharmawijaya
My Village 27
Colours of Illusion 28
There Still Exists 29
The Eternal Peasant 29

Firdaus Abdullah
Song for Sariyati.. 31
Waiting for One Who Waits 32
Return To Me 33
Five Thoughts At Five Stops 33

Kassim Ahmad
Dialogue 36
Your Poet... 37
Wanderer's Journey 38
A Pact... 40
Assembly of Souls... 41

Kemala
Ocean.. 43
See 44
In the Distance 45
That Love, My Beloved 46
Quatrain of January 47
December ii 47
The Room 48
Coral... 48

Latiff Mohidin
Dream I.. 50
Mirror 51
The Puppeteer's Wayang... 51
Words Adrift on Air 52
The Legend of the Dawn 53
A City, A Grandmother and Death 53
His Thick Shroud... 54
The Shore of Time 55
Mask or My Name is Rawana.................................... 55

Lim Swee Tin
A Flute and That Old Man....................................... 57
Mirror I 58
Portrait of the xxth Century.................................... 58
Remembering.. 59
Pearl Poem 59

Moechtar Awang
Surrender I 60
Tok Bageh.. 61
Incantation of Origins.. 62
Season of Sorrow 63
A Message to a Wife (II) (for AS) 64

Muhammad Haji Salleh
Si Tenggang's Homecoming...................................... 65
Prologue 67
Chapter Twelve 70
Chapter Thirty-Two (ii) 71
The Teller of Tales 75
Sailor 75

Rahman Shaari
In Turn 77
Yellow Carpet 78
The Old Woman and Her Dog 79
Drought 80
Let It Be 80
Outside the Group 81

Siti Zainon Ismail
Sleeping Platform 82
In the Curve of the Taj 83
Siti Melorinda 84
Rainbow 85
Mogul Night Flute-Music 85
4th December 1985 86
The Flute Player 87
Prayer 87

T. Alias Taib
Prostitute 4 89
Rat Race 90
A Push Cart 90
My World 91
Apple 92
Secret 92
Drought 93
Keys 93

Usman Awang
Voice from the Grave 95
Black Snow 97
Beloved 98
Under the Shadow of Red Tulips 99
Father Utih 100
Greetings to the Continent 101
The Times 102
Letter from the Bird Community to the Mayor 102
Little Girl 104
Can Mother Crab Teach her Young to Walk Straight? 105

Wan A. Rafar
Bagong 106
A Couple of Bodies 107
Stone 108
Without You 109

Zaihasra
The Ocean at Dawn 110
Here Time Wounds a Love that Fades 111
A Moment Put to the Test 112
My City 113

Zurinah Hassan
In an Aquarium 114
The Other Love Poem 115
With the Earth's Dust 115

Looking for Space 116
Marriage 116
Are You Still Playing Your Flute 117
Certainty.. 118
Waves at My Feet Waves in My Heart....................... 118
Life from a Train Window 119

PREFACE

This anthology of modern Malaysian poetry was undertaken by Dewan Bahasa dan Pustaka Malaysia to introduce and promote important poems by Malaysian poets to an international audience.

Most of the poems included have been awarded the annual Malaysian National Literary Prize (1971–89) and are translated by Professor Dr Muhammad Haji Salleh (who also contributes the Introduction to this anthology). He is Head of the Malay Studies Department of the National University of Malaysia, as well as a critic and editor – he has published 13 books, including *Tradition and Change in Contemporary Malay–Indonesian Poetry* (1977), *Selections from Contempory Malaysian Poetry* (1978), *The Travel Journals of Si Tenggang II* (1979) and *An Anthology of Contemporary Malaysian Literature* (1988).

We would like to thank Mr Harry Aveling (Hafiz Arif), a former lecturer at University of Science Malaysia, Pulau Pinang, and Writer in Residence at Dewan Bahasa dan Pustaka, for his invaluable assistance in translating some of the poems here.

The third translator is Adibah Amin (formerly well known as an editor and journalist at *The New Straits Times*, as a novelist and as a scriptwriter). Adibah and Hafiz were awarded the Anugerah Pengembangan Sastra ESSO–GAPENA in 1991 for their role in promoting Malay literature internationally.

The other translators are Nor Aini Osman, Ahmad Kamal Abdullah and Dr Barclay M. Newman (formerly a professor of Greek Studies at William College, Missouri, USA). Dr Newman has translated *Modern Malaysian Stories* (1977), *Modern Malaysian Poetry* (1980), and *Crisis* (a novel by Alias Ali, 1974).

Last but not least we would like to express our gratitude to the Directors of In Print for their invaluable idea for a co-publication project between Dewan Bahasa dan Pustaka and In Print. In this way, we hope that foreign readers will have a glimpse of the Malay literary and cultural world. Our thanks also to Ayob Yamin and A. Rahim Abdullah for compiling this book.

Dato' Haji Jumaat bin Dato' Haji Mohd Noor
Director General,
Dewan Bahasa dan Pustaka,
Kuala Lumpur

January 1992

MODERN MALAYSIAN POETRY: AN INTRODUCTION

Muhammad Haji Salleh

Apart from some collections of oral *penglipur lara* (tales for 'entertainment of the sorrowful') and some love *pantuns*, traditional (and classical) Malay literature was and is quite obviously involved in the real life and values of its society. A poem was composed to fulfil certain functions, some didactic but others for the more practical use of shamans, ceremonies and rituals, and even for lullabies. Literature was born from these needs and was not to be divorced from them, from the concept of usefulness and some form of involvement. The poet or *pujangga*, to use the old term, was in his traditional society a learned man, among its more fortunate members and often its elder. From him were demanded ideas, interpretation of political, social and religious phenomena, and moral guidance. He had no choice but to be the elder and to contribute accordingly to his community.

In this society, the welfare of the community overrides that of the individual. When society was ruled according to feudalistic principles, the individual, especially the peasant, was no more than a serf to his lord, unlettered and knowing little of his personal rights or the need for a change in the system. He was suppressed – and the above constraints made the rise of the individual almost impossible.

So literature and the arts were moulded within the strict conventions, systems and values of the society. One convention was that literary forms were already fixed, and consequently stable. Whatever changes were effected had to be executed within these conventions. Talent and individual genius concentrated on the creation of the striking image and on technical devices for its allusion, music, and the overall fineness of the poem or story. It was only within these bounds that the author was free to show his ability and uniqueness. The internal formal development of the *pantun* from an independent and self-sufficient quatrain into a six or eight or ten line verse form, or the ingenious linked *pantun* (known as the *pantoum* in French), illustrates how a radical talent may change a time-honoured form. However, this was still done within a strict tradition.

Individual talent, then, worked within very strict conditions and conventions. It had to carve out little unique pictures within the hard and fragile ivory of the *pantun*. However, when a significant new poem was composed, as is illustrated by the thousands of good poems that have been passed down through the centuries, it was preserved by later generations.

When the modern poets began to write, in the late 1920s or 1930s, a strong sense of literary convention, tradition and social involvement was evident in their poems. The process of loosening these old ties to make a new poetry was to take a long time, and it is still being carried out. With this loosening of ties too, poets began to discover their individual talents and tried to blend them with forms already accepted as capable of providing greater opportunity for personal expression. This introduction attempts to trace the development of Malaysian poetry through the awakening of the self and the process of individualization.

I would like to look at the works of several major Malaysian poets. Among them I would include Usman Awang, A. Samad Said, Kassim Ahmad, Baha Zain, Latiff Mohidin and Kemala. I will also try to look at the directions taken by T. Alias Taib, Rahman Shaari, Wan A. Raffar, Moechtar Awang, Zurinah Hassan, Siti Zainon Ismail, Mansor Md Saman and Lim Swee Tin.

The larger social comitment than merely the individual world and the personal perspective may be traced in the numerous poems published in books, periodicals and news-papers. Here, it is useful to analyse the concept and use of theme, the new poetic forms and modes of language favoured by these poets.

Themes

A functional concept of literature, inherited from the oral and classical past, still had a strong hold on the literary mind of the writers of the 1930s and 1940s. This concept naturally continued when modern literature was born. New novels and poems took the functional, or more particularly, the didactic stance and structure of the past. Writers still saw themselves as among the more fortunate members of society (indeed they were the 'educated' of the times, working as teachers or journalists) and voluntarily carried on their shoulders the burden of educating their less fortunate readers. In the 1950s this commitment became the official philosophy of a group of writers who called themselves Angkatan Sasterawan '50 (ASAS '50 or the 1950s Movement Writers). The arts were to serve society or, in their own words, *Seni Untuk Masyarakat* (Arts for the People). This extended the traditional concept of literature as directly involved in the life of society, sensitive to its needs and in many instances also its guide.

The ASAS '50 saw its writers as living in a wider world and equipped with a sense of contemporary reality and knowledge. They were involved in the predicament of their race, in the language, literature, culture, economy and the intricate whole of its life.[1] These writers saw, with little doubt, that literature was an instrument which could be used against the British colonial government, its political power and economic grip on the country. It was eloquently used to illustrate the pathetic situation in the Malay Peninsula, where the local people were no more than labourers for British or European companies and estates. Keris Mas (Kamaluddin Muhammad) and Usman Awang sketch clear pictures of exploitation in estates, factories and firms in their attempts to create further awareness among their readers.

After Independence in 1957, Usman Awang continued to write poems and plays with the same sense of commitment – though now his literature was an instrument for criticism and checking governmental or political excesses and injustice. Usman and his ASAS colleagues had many followers: in fact there was not a single important poet in the 1960s who did not feel that it was his or her moral duty to speak on behalf of the society he or she came from.

Usman has written with an empathy for the small man in the street, the factory worker on strike, the small-time hawker driven away from her spot on the five-foot way, the blacks in the US fighting for their rights, and the poor helpless peasants. All these themes add up to a major commitment to humanity itself along the lines of the ASAS '50 manifesto. Often enough Usman crosses racial and national boundaries to speak of peace, cooperation, and the need to live together in a world which is becoming progressively smaller.

Listen, for example, to Usman describing the fate of Pak Utih, the old peasant bound to a patch of dry land and an age-old poverty. In the last lines he juxtaposes him with the minister going away (from him?) in his limousine:

> He has one wife – whom he embraces until death
> five children who want to eat every day
> an old hut where an inherited tale is hanging
> a piece of barren land to cultivate.
>
> . . . .
>
> But malaria comes hunting them
> even though he offers a million prayers
>
> . . . .
>
> Father Utih still waits in prayer
> where are the leaders going in their limousines?

The poet suffers along with Pak Utih, giving him a voice he never had and dramatizing his problem, which in the poem has been transformed into one that Malaysians must solve together.

A. Samad Said, emerging onto the literary scene in the late 1950s, continued with this stance and commitment. Like his novels and stories, many of his early poems describe the bombed-out world of the Singapore poor. In the historically important poem '*Liar di Api*' ('Wild in the Fire'), the whole human race lives now in the rubble, agonizing over the memory of two past wars and overcome by images of the one to come. Yet Samad lived in two worlds. Writing during the years of the struggle for independence, he was often bouyed up by hopes of a new world, a new country independent and bestowing dignity on the Malaysian. Thus in another poem we see on a wide canvas, full of colour, the ship of independence being awaited by maidens on the beach, a beautiful symbolic painting of hope and a new world. At the same time, Kassim Ahmad, then a socialist, wrote sharply critical poems evaluating the country, its choice of lifestyle, its parliament and the role of the writers in such a country. Abandoning any romantic pose, he wrote with new intellectual and critical vigour.

Baha Zain (Baharuddin Zainal), the poet–critic, writing in the early 1960s, was initially fired by a desire for radical change of mind and ways. He saw the need for Malaysia to modernize, but yet was always aware that in this country the surface or the glitter is often taken for the real thing, without real understanding or belief.

For Baha, the poet is the social critic. His poetry shows him standing on the streets of the city to comment on what it has done to him or his neighbours. This is how he judges the city:

the city's feet are the wilderness
its nerves barbed wires
old, rusty and infected with tetanus
that bite into movement and vision
in the smoke of dust and soot
shattering the clarity
of ph.d minds, talents and personalities
become victims in the day's tangle
the repetition of life's routine
the white morning to wake up in
then to prostrate before a dark poisonous night.

this city is a den for grand planners
each to his own lot and direction
programming precise steps
adding – multiplying numbers on a bank card
analysing telex news of a coup d'etat
libel suits of politicians against editors
tracker dogs from a news office
morphine pushers in the coffee house
and everyone recognises the sweet smile of the beer waitress
the receptionist, dancer and florist
as temporary cures
for all that irritates
and hastens anger.

No hero, he is a man merely trying to survive in a complicated modern jungle that attempts to strangle him.

The younger poets who began writing in 1960s, like Kemala, Dharmawijaya, Firdaus Abdullah, Wahab Ali, among others, were no less socially oriented in their works. Like Usman they hoped that poetry could serve society.

The social or public poem is a very important sub-genre in modern Malaysian poetry. Even a poet like Latiff Mohidin, usually known for his graphic and imagistic experiments, addresses social problems in some poems, illustrating this all-important concept that poetry serves society.

The poets of the 1970s and 1980s are natural descendants of 1960s poets, who were in turn the direct descendants of the ASAS '50. For almost all of them, writers must speak of their society. Listen to what Zurinah Hassan, a young woman poet, says of her poetry in the earlier years of her literary career:

As you may see in my earlier poems, those written in 1967, 1968 and 1969 have social themes, especially those concerning peasants and fishermen. At that time I was deeply interested in being a social critic. Poems that have the people's suffering as their main theme may be seen in the third part of *Sesayup Jalan*. In those years, for example, if I saw padi fields I would recall poor peasants . . . I was also very interested in world events, its wars and famine.[2]

Zurinah was no outsider rebelling against 1970s literary thinking. She was putting on paper what many other Malaysian writers and audiences demanded of literature. This concept gave the young and older writer alike not only a sense of purpose, but also of function and direction. The writer became a man or woman bigger than his or her own personal world.

Zurinah cited many examples of her social themes and her commitment to her less fortunate fellow Malaysians. For example, the poem '*Rebolusi*' ('Revolution'):

> Sighs across the bunds
> are continually heard
> struggles for survival scratch hard
> at a bowl of rice
> over a possibility that often fades away.
>
> The water of Md. Saman's canal is muddy
> peasants are weak and buffaloes tired

in the festival of strength and belief
waiting for the moon to shine.

The tethered boat is wrecked by the monsoon
poverty bites into bodies
a month by the bamboo
he is abandoned by his fate.

What is awaited
are the sparks of revolution
on an earth less dry than the Sahara
on a sea without the mad winds
that so hopes for peace.

The call is for change, even for a revolution – which here is not clearly defined. But what is clear is the commitment to the suffering and struggles of the peasants.

Although the social involvement of her poems is quite overwhelming we do find personal perspectives and viewpoints on the problems that she raises. In the later poems especially, we no longer read of generalized scenes of poverty and suffering, rather we are given pictures painted through the more personal eyes of a keen and sensitive observer. Listen to this description for example:

the honourable leader
rides around towns and villages
to visit his people
people who are always hoping
many came out to welcome him
some were seriously ill.

and those stretched out
became more serious
more restless
disturbed by the loud sirens
of the limousine of the leader.

The personal idiom and cynicism are proofs of a personal perspective. As much as one hears the influence of Usman's *Pak Utih* one hears also Zurinah's tone, marking it with her own expression and voice.

What we see in Zurinah we also find in another young poet from Kelantan, Wan A. Raffar. The desire to write from one's own heart and personality has spread rapidly among the poets of the 1970s and 1980s and has become something that they have sought after. Wan A. Raffar, for example, writes:

> When the fire broke out
> they sought a place of safety
> they said
> oh you woman with flowing hair
> let's shelter at the roots of your hair.
>
> When things became worse
> they looked at each other
> then jumped into
> each other's eyes
> and closed them securely.
>
> At last they were safe
> in the only tear
> that falls onto the woman's cheek.

This poem does not take its theme from an individual experience but rather from a shared life, the need to shelter the insecure even though one has to grieve for it. It is a theme of sacrifice and social sharing. In his way, Wan A. Raffar is loyal to the concept of commitment of ASAS '50. However, the eyes that he looks through are not those of Usman Awang, but his own. He does not look on the general economic squalor of the 1950s, but finds a smaller area that is more intimately experienced, more personally felt and interpreted.

This reality has the colour of the personal, though in a more social sense. The observer is not transparent, as in the poems of Usman Awang or Masuri S.N. He is present in his poems as the unique maker and arranger of personal imagery that combines to give both a personal and social meaning.

In another poem, 'Advice of a Mother to a Bachelor Son', the poet, tongue-in-cheek, gives voice to the mother. She advises,

> You must marry, son, before you're 40
> because in our community
> 40 is too late.
> Are you afraid of women?
> If you wish

> I'll find the girl next door
> or in the village, there
> perhaps you want an English-educated one?

Here again the stance of the writer is no longer that of the preacher or eloquent speaker, but one who modestly or quietly looks upon life and comments on it. The treatment of the theme is very personal, the tone partly humorous. Yet we know that it is a social picture, but painted with the poet's own brush, colours and tone.

T. Alias Taib, too, is personal in his approach to social themes. Quoting Vincente Huldobro, 'may verse be like a key that opens a thousand doors', for example, he sees poetry as an act of opening doors to reality and therefore personally understanding it better. He finds a world that *he* knows well or is continually discovering. Thus, the centre of the world is the poet himself:

> with a bunch of keys at my feet
> i enter the maze of a thousand doors
> filled with lamentation and expectation of
> desperation
> one such tale of a labourer one evening
> the drain he was sweeping
> the dry leaves fragments of his life
> bits and pieces of the future
> prayers of friends thrown asunder

The quotation and the poem read like a creative statement on the function of poetry – one that opens for the poet a real world, but one with a slant for the destitute, the poor and the helpless. T. Alias Taib writes with a strong sense of commitment, which in his case is for the poor and against the minister (in '*Menteri*', 'Minister') who liberally promises the villagers new bridges or roads or schools for the village.

Both 'Keys' and 'Minister' are more public in their tone and delivery. They have more similarities with those of ASAS '50 writers. However, like the other poets we have discussed earlier, at the opposite end to his social poems we find T. Alias Taib himself, the private poet looking at 'pieces of fate' or 'fragments of the future', small fragments of a big world, from personal perspectives. Listen to this observation, for example:

> the sun sprinkles its powder
> on to the padi fields' tongue
>
> the clouds roll on, restless
> in its heart
> the winds break
>
> the winds yawn
> in the mouth of a buffalo
> in thunder is stranded
>
> silence and drought smoke
> between the brown leaves
> it does not rain
>
> a dune stretches
> in the grey heart
> of a peasant
>
> the sun sprinkles
> over the throat of a village.

Quieter, and perhaps coming from a desire to communicate in a less public way, the poem is more subtle, drawing its strength from the poet's responses to the lengthening drought. This is the personal colouring that is so important in the committed or social poems of Alias Taib and the most recent poets.

Moechtar Awang, a young Kelantanese, surprised the Malaysian literary scene by winning second prize of the 1980 international Puisi Putra award (for poetry in the Malay–Indonesian language). His book of poems, *Pasrah* ('Surrender'), is essentially made up of the winning poems that have at their core a religious view of life, surrender to Allah. In these works we are guided by Moechtar's religious piety and principles. His reductions of the great religious values to personal experiences, thoughts and feelings is a new and dramatic move in contemporary Malaysian poetry. In *'Pasrah i'* ('Surrender I') the voice is a quiet prayer:

a clot of silence
a quiver in the bowels of the night
suddenly falls onto a mirror
sprinkling the fragrance of frangipani
to the area around mother's cemetery
my hands the soft silk
as though arranging velvet
reaching for Your heaven
that hushes all secrets
suddenly
my odorous and dirty face kneels
at the doors of Your ears
then to say a million prayers
prayers of freedom from sin
prayers of freedom from revenge
prayers full of regret
prayers that request a million forgiveness.

Moechtar finds a richness of theme in the religious and has continued to write about it. However, it seems that this theme was preceded by a group of social poems. In the commentary on *Pasrah*, Jeniri Amir says that in the first section of the book, called '*Siput dan Jerami*' ('Sea Shells and Straw'), the poet deals mostly with the fate of the peasants, the rubber tappers, the trishaw peddlars, manual labourers, and the petty traders.[3] He is of the opinion that this section is a record of the poet's sympathy for this group of people in their confrontation with fate, especially that which comes in the form of natural destroyers – the monsoon and drought.

Again, the social issues are part of this poet's work. Even without analysing these poems one is able to see that he is following in the concept and function of a traditional writer. In this sense the religious may be seen as part of the social, because in the practice of Malay poetry the religious is public, rather than private. It is open, discussed in the abstract, and generally pontifical or missionary in nature. But Moechtar has reduced this tradition to a quiet one that describes his individual religious experiences in a collection of clear personal imagery.

Rahman Shaari, now teaching at the University of Malaya, is also a poet of ideas – one who finds that the external world helps him to new insights and ideas arising from a personal

interaction with this world. In the poem '*Perbandingan*'
('Comparison'), he observes the irony of human action and
thought, where we are often defeated by our very own
arguments and we become receivers while at the same time
acting as contributors. He concludes that we must recognize
defeat when we are defeated and accept victory when we are
triumphant. We should take life as it flows around us rather
than fight it.

Returning home to Perlis, he often notices that, while he is
still in love with the beautiful padi lands, he has also brought
home new ways and is looking through new eyes. This is the
irony and the conflict which he carries within himself:

> On the verandah
> my eyes are bathed in the ocean of padi
> a yellow carpet
> you have flowed through my culture
> a bosom friend who has once parted
> returning to knock on the door of my conscience
>
> I have now returned to you
> with the old undying love
> I return with old emotions
> and a new mind.

As we go through the poems, the worlds and minds of these
young poets, we notice a certain progression into a more
personal and internal universe. In the above discussion, I have
attempted to trace their roots and show how closely they were
related to social or public poetry – but I was careful, I hope,
also to show that all reflect a personal slant or approach. In the
poems of Siti Zainon Ismail and Lim Swee Tin, especially in
the latter's earlier works, the social world recedes, leaving us
with the labyrinth of the poet's emotions and experiences.
These are strange sketches of the self that we have seldom read
about.

Thus in Siti Zainon's first book of poems, *Nyanyian Malam*
('*Night Melodies*'), there is a predominance of images created
from the world of emotions, which, though obscure in their
association, are clearly related to her own psychological life.
The world that she brings to her readers is deeply personal,
and most communicates with us when it follows a more

ordinary logic. Otherwise its images tend to become correlatives of her personal life, friendships and artistic interests. *'Profil Cinta'* ('Profile of Love'), for example, throws onto the page beautiful sketches of a dancer who is so full of a love which can defeat both the evil god Rawana and the gigantic bird Jentayu:

> How elegant
> the curved finger of a slender maiden
> in the night of the dance
> she reaches out with her hands
> her slender neck
> flowing hair the *cempaka* fragrance
> how perfect a pair of calves
> glittering nails
> in sweet light.
>
> Fingers and nails
> her heart, eyes mournful
> she's my Sita
> like a wave in the dance.

The images are characteristically Zainon's, taken from her myriad artistic encounters, thick with emotional associations. They mirror, or are in fact fragments of a soul, an aesthete's beautiful view of her private world.

Like Siti Zainon's, Lim Swee Tin's first book *Eva* gathers for us images of his internal world, here made up mostly of different emotional states, situations and aspects of his love-life. They seem to be all-consuming, cutting out altogether the social world. The whole book may be read as a long poem of this love. As an illustration, let us choose *'Sajak untuk Eva'* ('Poem for Eva'). It is very private and refers to a world within:

> returning to the room
> there was a
> scent of newly burnt wax
>
> the colour of twilight that merges
> in your eyes
> is still
> flitting on leaves
> of my day

> and the sorrow
> is still hidden, eva,
> behind your hair.

In their later works Zainon and Lim are less personal and
therefore more communicative, but their worlds are markedly
more private when compared to their contemporaries. These
poems are coloured by an imagination that recreates the less
pretty pictures of reality. If we juxtapose them with the more
social or even political poems of Usman Awang, they may be
seen as a product of a kind of neo-romanticism, where the
individual has learnt to appreciate his or her own personal
emotions and to sketch them on paper – an act which has
seldom found encouragement in the Malaysian literary scene.

As we look back to the young poets we notice that their
themes range from the public to the very personal. However,
in all the poets the sense of the self, the individual personality
has progressively found a presence and a natural expression,
never before seen or heard in modern Malaysian poetry. The
Malaysian individual as poet has come of age, and may even be
quite healthy as the poets have not gone to extremes in
speaking only of themselves or worse still of their paranoia.
There is often a sure sense of both the self and social
commitment. The world is balanced in the poems and the
mind that looks at it.

Poetic forms as moulds of a new world

The free verse form which evolved in Europe at the beginning
of the twentieth century was undoubtedly a product of a new
development in individual liberty, a higher status of the
individual in society and a post-Freudian discovery of the self.
The poetic forms of nineteenth-century Europe were loosened
to allow the expression of a more deeply personal voice of the
poet, in a breath and rhythm more natural to himself or
herself. Thus it represented more closely the honest reaction of
the poet.

There was a supporting social situation that helped the
individual to grow into himself or herself. And the social
context was doubtless very important in shaping or misshaping
the structure of poetry.

When the Malay poets of the 1930s tried to experiment with this free verse form, it was with a certain blurred vision of what it really was and a pain of confrontation with their own tradition. Unlike their Western models and predecessors they had no ready-made social situation and clear progress of the status of the individual so that they could easily break into a form as individual as free verse. They had only a desire to deviate from the older moulds and a burning youthful rebellion. They thus had to imitate a situation – a mood and an intellectual atmosphere that was outside themselves and far, far away in Europe.

The act of understanding and writing real free verse took a long time; in fact until the social situation could catch up with this individual form and the individual was really free. The 1970s and 1980s may be said to have been a period when the form was finally mastered and used naturally to parallel the poet's social situation and individual rights. No longer were the strong personal choices of the poets reduced by poetic forms of the past. Now, the new form, experimented with for at least 40 years, has come to be a natural medium for modern Malaysian poetry.

Although the poets of the 1930s began to break the traditional lines of the *pantun* and *syair*, it was in the 1950s that we saw the real beginning of a continuous experimentation with the new form that later became the modern *sajak*, or Malaysian free verse.

Masuri S.N., with Usman Awang, initially tried to change the tone of the poet's voice. The former used a louder and firmer tone, while Usman varied the traditional gentle sounds with traces of indignation or criticism. Slowly, the tone of the new poetry became more varied and natural.

Beginning with the clear echoes of the *pantun* and the *syair* in the late 1940s, Usman Awang slowly experimented with the *verse libre*, bringing his Malay forms to merge with the new European form. His earlier attempts took him more than a decade. Yet, however much he has sought change, Usman's form, metaphor and melody are always recognizably Malay. Take, for example, these opening verses of *'Gadis Kecil'* ('Little Girl'):

> Her body reminded me of
> the areca palm in quiet country
> tall and thin
> in heavy storms
> broken branches fall around
> but the palm stands erect
> awaiting the morning sun.
>
> So it was with this little girl
> thin as areca palm
> year after year meeting his father
> across the barbed wire of a prison
> imprisoned these many years
> courageously fighting oppression
> steady and faithful.

The lines and verses are almost regular in length. The general rhythm harkens back to the old forms. The images from nature foreshadow the prison, just as the primary image of the *pantun* always foreshadows the meaning proper.

A. Samad Said, who was in quite close contact with international writing through his English language background, began to experiment early in his career. In fact, his early works were milestones in the progress of the *sajak* form that forever radically changed the concept of the Malay poem on paper. He broke the regular verses and lines, and gave them the irregular face of the 1960s and 1970s. The poem '*Liar di Api*', for example, used some of the techniques of page lay-out, no doubt from his experience as a journalist. This is quite different from Kassim Ahmad's poetry, which is a clear break with the past. Kassim's lines are short and the verses are bare without decoration. They zoom into their subject without ceremony.

Baha Zain, in turn, advanced the graphic form further, giving it its fragmented face. Thus when he chose the 'collage' for a mould to describe the new urban life, it was the best choice of forms. Through it, he could juxtapose unceremoniously art and imitation, the new symbols of modernization and technology and the pretence to international sophistication. The poem '*Kolej "Gerakan Moden"* ' ('The "Modern Movement" Collage') is worth quoting in full for its new and lasting significance:

petrol fumes, tractor smoke
flats, massage parlours
women & hotel = prostitute
mascara, eye-shadow = floor show
(Beware of Dogs) bungalow
aquarium & orchid, poodle & piano
antique chairs, classical music
status + symbol = modern − progressive
'cheap sale' at the new supermarket

invitation card
reception
R.S.V.P.
tel.: 8891
lounge suit
cocktails
b.g. ale
whisky soda
et cetera

in a city lane
the artist asks for directions
looking for a gallery
to exhibit his collage

a collector
buys his painting
and in the grand hall
hangs a false collage.

Latiff Mohidin, a poet–painter, employed both his talents in his poetry. Trained in art, he was more sensitive to lines, shapes and colours. All his poems reflect this. Latiff's early poems were small imagistic works, essential in form and organization. They were often very concentrated, leaving out all decorative inessentials. The beauty of his works is to be found in the tight-knit of the different parts, the sharp images and the minimal aesthetics. Take, for example, the poem '*Pohon Cemara*' ('Waiting'). The close repetition of the lines of the first verse in the second is done with a very fine sense of symmetry. The small changes that he includes in the symmetry are developments that must be sought and quietly compared with those of the preceding verse:

casuarina tree
dies awaiting
north wind
at river's edge
north wind
at day's end

old crow
awaiting death
casuarina tree
at river edge
casuarina tree
at finger's end.

Latiff's later poetry returns to the metaphorical core of the Malay allegorical tradition. Parables woven in the prose-poem fit well with the allusions that Malays of old revelled in.

Firdaus Abdullah, Dharmawijaya, and, to some extent, Kemala were sensitive to the traditional forms. Like Usman Awang, they used not only the forms from the past but also the various technical devices of oral literature in repetition, in natural images and in regular verses and lines. They were a popular group of Malay 'romantic' poets and in their use of tradition struck chords in those Malay readers who also were steeped in the old poetic traditions.

Thus when the poets of the 1970s and 1980s sat down to write their poems, the form that was chosen to mould their emotions and thoughts was free verse. There was no other alternative – this is the Malaysian form, used by their predecessors, their own contemporaries and the poets themselves.

We can consider the 1970s and 1980s as a further stage in the process of maturing the new verse form into a personal poetic medium. There were many approaches to it. On the one hand, there was a feeling among some writers that the genres of the past are valuable assets that grew from Malay and Malaysian roots and should be re-used for a more distinctive mode for the modernizing Malaysian. For example, Moechtar Awang experimented with acknowledged lessons from traditional literature. The most frequent traditional form that has appeared in his works, in one form or another, is the *mantera*, or the incantatory charm used in folk healing. The speaking voice used in this form is often dramatic and rhetorical. The genre is used to command spirits to leave the bodies of the shaman's patients and to strengthen confidence and spiritual power. Thus we see in Moechtar's '*Tok Bageh*' an eloquent and commanding voice:[4]

> prepare me
> tumeric rice
> from a million fields
> betel-nut leaves
> from a million plants
> prepare me
> the fragrance in incense
> from every corner
> well water
> from a million districts
> prepare me
> farm eggs
> prepare me
> copper needles
>
> . . . .
>
> I will rise
> with the soul of the earth
> I will run
> with the soul of the lightning
> I will shout
> with the soul of the thunder
> I am the guardian
> of all forests
> I am the healer
> of all diseases
> I come
> from the blue skies.

Of course this is not a new *mantera* in traditional clothes. Although one often hears the cadence of the traditional form, it is in fact a modern poem with lessons learnt and used from the *mantera* of the past. The individual is pushed to the forefront to command spirits, diseases and forests. He is a superman. He is also the mask of the poet, speaking of his individuality, the modern factor that has transformed the old form. A similar process takes place in the Indonesian poet Chairil Anwar's 'Story for Dien Tamaela'.

The *mantera* and other traditional oral forms also preserve a number of narrative techniques that have attracted our young poets. The heavily oral mode of parallelism seems to be a favourite of Moechtar and Wan Raffar. However, here the similarity between them ends, as they go their separate ways in their experiments. While Moechtar's *mantera* is fairly rhetorical and tight, Wan Raffar tries to loosen it a little to accommodate his personality, though not to a speaking voice. I quote a few lines from *'Bagong'* as an example of his use of the *mantera*:

> I am bagong
> bagong seri alas
> from the copper mountains
> alone with life-breath
> I am bagong
> descended from the gods
> watched over by the gods.

This *mantera* deals more with self-definition, describing Bagong as he sees himself, in the language of a god. Again, it reminds us of Chairil Anwar's poem 'Story for Dien Tamaela' in its employment of a mask for the poet's real self.

Siti Zainon too finds a wealth of models and examples in traditional literature. Like the traditional artist, she looks upon poetry as a thing of musical and visual beauty. Zainon is in fact a modern aesthete, enjoying the liquid cadences of the Malay language. Her poems are songs of the soul or the senses, full of colour and personal insight.

Her poetic form is likewise heavily influenced by this concept of composition. In it, the musical organization becomes very significant. This is further enhanced by musical devices of rhymes, alliteration, parallelism, repetition and heavy assonance.

Zainon's great advantage over her contemporaries is that she is also a visual artist (oil painting and pen sketches) and she has made full use of this to bring over images of her world, with great flair and colour, though not necessarily in a unified whole.

Lim Swee Tin's poetry has some similarities with that of

Zainon. Both are musical and romantic in their basic moods. However, while Zainon's poems have traditional roots Lim's are more modern and individual.

There is another group of poets who try, on the other hand, to bring their poetic forms closer to the speaking voice, copying its rhythm and even looseness. Very much less musical or imagistic, they are significantly more direct and prosaic. Perhaps this choice has a great deal to do with their themes and obsessions.

Between the musical and the loose conversational forms are the poems of T. Alias Taib, Rahman Shaari, and (sometimes) Wan A. Rafar. They seem to have found personal voices and forms for their individual needs. These forms seem to have been created from a sense of the past, the traditional modes of expressions, and lessons from their immediate predecessors like Baha Zain and Latiff Mohidin.

Thus T. Alias Taib has a recognizable formal style, using fairly short lines, compact but also quite conversational. He finds virtue in the regularity of breath and arranges his verses quite consciously. These qualities contribute to a stable form that also embodies light musical elements. *'Penemuan'* ('Discovery') is a case in point:

> two women
> hypnotised and moved
> found life's secrets
> in voices of my poems
>
> I who live
> without secrets
> wrote down those lines
> unconsciously.

Like T. Alias Taib's, Rahman Shaari's lines are short and compact. He sometimes uses rhymes but in a more relaxed and informal way. Unlike T. Alias his verses are seldom regular. They tend to follow the conversational structure of speech. These few lines from *'Jarak'* ('Distance') illustrate my point:

> A half day with you
> I found a chain of worries
> that's you, it seems?

> Who's wrong?
> your youthful gaiety seems almost lost
> behind the year's curtain
>
> Who is the interpreter of love
> to reduce the distance between our speech?

In general, one notices that the form has been mastered with distinct characteristics bestowed by the poets' personalities and styles. All of them are part of the free verse tradition, though many may feel that their own Malay genres can contribute to it. The form has been made as flexible as possible for individual needs. There is little of the extremism of concrete poetry. I honestly feel there is a maturity of choice and a combination of different elements from diverse sources. However, this stability, on the other hand, illustrates also a conservatism that is healthy for the moment, but needs change in the next few years.

Language and personality

The language of Malay poetry is often a gentle mellifluous language, rich in vocals and thus inordinately smooth in its flow. The Malay poetic aesthetics of harmony demand that the writer weave his lines and verses so that there are no verbal notches, no staccato sounds and no gravelly surfaces. This produces beautiful love poems – of which of course the *pantuns* are the most well-known.

Usman Awang is a master of the Malay language who listens to it under its surfaces, and within its syllables. His tone is gentle. Yet like Usman the man, his anger and protest must be read behind his voice, in his words, beyond his rhythm. I quote the last verse of his 'Letter from the Bird Community to the Mayor':

> Lord Mayor,
> this letter requests that in your wisdom
> you will protect each branch, each root,
> each leaf, each petal, each bower,
> for these have been our homes through the centuries,
> and it would also be for the good of man,
> his health and happiness, his peace and mind,

to let nature and its myriad beauties bloom
in the brilliant sun.

Yet a harmoniously smooth language also belies the slowly
fragmenting society, quite harsh in its new ways. When
Kassim Ahmad and Baha Zain wrote in the 1960s they had to
give new sinews to their medium. The muscles are not only for
their physical sounds but also for their intellectual discursive
quality. Listen to Kassim distinguishing his poet from the
romantic:

> *Penyairmu*
> *darinya dipinta keindahan*
> *lagu dari hati tenteram*
> *harmonis dengan alam.*

> *Penyairku*
> *pondoknya di pinggir kali*
> *luas hatinya merangkum dunia*
> *bertafakur tentang untungnya.*

> Of your poet
> you demand
> songs from a serene heart
> in harmony with the world

> My poet –
> his heart by the stream
> his heart embracing the wide world
> meditates upon his situation.

Baha Zain further advanced the Malay poetic language as used
in a newly industrialized country. Bombarded by the new
industrialization and a harsher environment, the poetic language too must reflect these new developments. True to
himself, Baha experimented with his voice and tone in the
many different poems that we have included in this anthology.

Firdaus, Dharmawijaya, Kemala, and A. Wahab Ali on the
other hand follow the traditional path, much like Usman
Awang. They find virtue and melody in the sweet sounds of
the language, thus continuing a long tradition. Rhymes, the
beautiful word and traditional images give their poems the

traditional beauty that they revere as the ideal. Listen to Dharmawijaya, for example, in 'My Village':

>the fountain of my love, my village
>how have you fared
>laterite roads
>hennaed with dust
>its fields and swamps
>in drought, often.
>
>the land of longing, my village
>young children
>are grown and adult
>patiently begging
>in the jaws of sorrow
>and its festival
>bathing in the sunshine
>adrift alone.

While discussing the themes and forms of these younger poets, I have also touched on the use of language and the tone employed in the various works. I need not repeat what I have written above. However, one thing is clear – these young poets have developed recognizable styles of their own, which is a great achievement, especially with very influential poets like Usman Awang, Baha Zain and Latiff Mohidin still around. In their works we no longer find the stiff '*pujangga*' or heroic prose of the 1950s or even the stance of the social fighter of the 1960s. Yet apart from Zainon and Lim Swee Tin, they all subscribe to a poetry of commitment. There is more humility in their lines, a result of a contemporary interpretation of reality.

As there is no one accepted language of poetry, and therefore no demand to use this single dialect, poets have felt free to mould styles for their own use out of their own voices and special ways of speaking. We hear a very much softer tone in the 1970s and 1980s and a more internal language. There is more hesitancy (a product of doubt), cynicism, and a closer observation of the shifting reality. The preferred style is the conversational, discursive, or the confessional that we see in the works of Zurinah and Rahman.

End note

Malaysian poetry moves into its future very cautiously, its poets always feeling secure with tradition and even including that tradition in their modern works. There is a sense of conservatism, and all experimentation is censored by this general mood.

Yet within this situation most of the poets discussed have found not only clear and recognizable voices, but have moulded forms that could carry these voices. The individual is now a natural part of the interpretation of reality, free verse is the chosen form and the tone of language used is natural. Poets have felt for some time now that it is important to speak as individuals and to find individual modes of expression.

The poets of the 1970s and 1980s are surer of themselves and the possibilities of poetry than were many of their predecessors.

References and bibliography

1. Syed Husin Ali, 'Asas '50 dan Cita-cita Kemasyarakatannya', in Muhammed Haji Salleh *et al*, *Warisan Asas '50*, Dewan Bahasa dan Pustaka, Kuala Lumpur, 1981, pp 21–23.
2. Zurinah Hassan, *Puisi dan Saya*, unpublished.
3. Jeniri Amir, '*Pasrah*: Pengucapannya begitu Natural', *Bintang Timur*, Penang, 13 June 1981.
4. Moechtar Awang, *Pasrah*, Dewan Bahasa dan Pustaka, Kuala Lumpur, 1981.

General references:
A.M. Thani, ed, *Esei Sastera Asas '50*, Dewan Bahasa dan Pustaka, Kuala Lumpur, 1982.
Muhammad Haji Salleh *et al*, *Tradition and Change in Contemporary Malay–Indonesian Poetry*, Penerbit Universiti Kebangsaan Malaysia, Bangi, 1977.
Muhammad Haji Salleh *et al*, *Warisan ASAS '50*, Dewan Bahasa dan Pustaka, Kuala Lumpur, 1981.

Poetry collections:
Dharmawijaya, ed, *Lagu Kehidupan: Antologi Puisi 25 Penyair*, Dewan Bahasa dan Pustaka, Kuala Lumpur, 1983.
Kemala, ed, *Kumpulan Puisi Malaysia, Malaysian Poetry, 1975–1985*, Dewan Bahasa dan Pustaka, Kuala Lumpur, 1988.
Lim Swee Tin, *Eva*, privately published, Kota Bharu, 1981.
Moechtar Awang, *Pasrah*, Dewan Bahasa dan Pustaka, Kuala Lumpur, 1981.
Rahman Shaari, *Hamparan Kuning*, Utusan, Kuala Lumpur, undated.

Siti Zainon Ismail, *Nyanyian Malam*, Dewan Bahasa dan Pustaka, Kuala Lumpur, 1976.

Siti Zainon Ismail, *Puisi Putih Sang Kekasih*, Universiti Kebangsaan Malaysia, Bangi, 1984.

T. Alias Taib, *Pemburu Kota*, Dewan Bahasa dan Pustaka, Kuala Lumpur, 1978.

T. Alias Taib, *Seberkas Kunci*, Dewan Bahasa dan Pustaka, Kuala Lumpur, 1985.

Zurinah Hassan, *Sesayup Jalan*, Penerbit Universiti Sains Malaysia, Penang, 1974.

Zurinah Hassan, *Di Sini Tiada Perhentian*, Pewarna, Kuala Lumpur, 1977.

THE PUPPETEER'S WAYANG

A selection of modern Malaysian poetry

A. GHAFAR IBRAHIM

Abdul Ghafar Ibrahim was born in Selangor in 1943. He was trained at the Teachers Training College before furthering his studies in Fine Arts in the USA. He obtained his MA Degree in Fine Arts from the University of Eastern Illinois. Abdul Ghafar currently teaches in the Faculty of Education at the National University of Malaysia. Ghafar is also an artist whose works have been exhibited in Belgium, Singapore, America, Australia and several other countries. Among his books are *Tan Sri Bulan* (1976), *Tak Tun* (1978), and *Yang Yang* (1986). Most of his works have been translated into English.

Age

age comes uninvited
suddenly arriving
in the rhythm of the waves.
age becomes part of you
locks the doors
and closes the windows
to the rainbow world.
the future is obvious.
morning:
    tick
       tock
       tick
    tock
the moon leaves,
night:
    tock
tick
tock

             tick
      the sun leaves.
      the calendar
      sheds its pages
                    one
             by
         one

      (*translated by Harry Aveling*)

House 28

i came from room 27
fresh ready full of faith
grim determination on my face
and filled the space and time
in my house house 28
with my sun
              me
and my moon
              me
and my new companion.
no one lives here
              apart from
us;
we are never afraid
strong by day
together at night
i open the window
          the sun rushes in
i wipe the sweat from my face
          the moon shines
it is never lonely.
strong by day
together at night
with the sun

         me
         and my new companion
and the moon
         me
         and my new companion
we are united in the search
for our us.

(*translated by Harry Aveling*)

Five Minutes to Now

in five minutes i will reach now
i will stand in front of her and try to forget last night
but i won't be able to, because of tomorrow
five minutes to now
now
i don't feel time passing
all i feel
is now
all i feel is last night
last night
all i feel is tomorrow
tomorrow
i don't feel me
time passes too quickly.
quickly
at the harbour
at the airport
at the train station
at the taxi rank
at the bus terminal.
time leaves too quickly
leaving
boat-train-plane-taxi-bus
are all leaving in five minutes

are all arriving in five minutes
five minutes is nothing
it won't feel like five minutes
it will feel like five seconds
it is faster than any five.
is anything faster than five –
the number five, five points or
time
time is faster than all the hours-minutes-seconds-moments-
instants

five minutes pass and the passengers
rest their chins on their hands or worry.
perhaps in the next five minutes
a poem will pass through my mind
and breathe five minutes, more or less
for me or for someone else.
in five minutes our blood will beat
or stop
and we may be able to love each other
for five minutes
or we may not
we may come to know each other in less than five minutes
we may able to refrain from our unintended enmity
in five times a day and a night
that is, in less than five minutes from now
five ecstatic moments of pure pleasure when i arrive.

(*translated by Harry Aveling*)

Old Man

an old man at home
Like a ruBber tree
O   R
N   O
E   K
L   E
Y   N
waiting
waiting

(*translated by Harry Aveling*)

My Lord Moon Kite

My Lord the Moon Kite riding freely
like a bird
wings smoothly opening like a flower
searching
taut silken jacket   shining sashes
lunging   flowing
kicking   roaring
parrying   shouting
ang-ngang-ngang-ngang

aung-ung-ung-ung

nnnggggggg

My Lord the Moon Kite
on high
like a bird.

(*translated by Harry Aveling*)

Crows

                              gak
                              gak
                        gak
                     gak
                  gak
               gak
gak
crows never pretend
that they enjoy singing
the noise helps them survive
the silence
gak
     gak
gak   gak
     gak   gak
          gak   gak
gak   gak   gak
     gak   gak   gak
          gak
                    gakkkkk
gakkkkkkk
picking the eyes
out of loneliness
as they melodiously search
for the truth
of hatred
akkk
     akkkk   aaaakkkkk
          akkkkk aaakkkk
                    aakkk

(*translated by Harry Aveling*)

A. SAMAD SAID

A. Samad Said was born on 9 April 1935 in Melaka. He received his primary and secondary education in Singapore. His first job was at the Singapore General Hospital for just six months. He then moved to Kuala Lumpur to work for the newspaper *Fikiran Rakyat*, returned to Singapore to work with *Utusan Zaman* before joining *Berita Harian* in Kuala Lumpur. He is now a freelance writer. He was conferred the Literary Pioneer Award on 29 May 1976. In 1979 he won the SEA Write Award in Bangkok and in 1986 was accorded the National Literary Award (Anugerah Sastera Negara). His work includes: short stories – *Liar di Api* and *Daun-duan Berguguran* (1962), *Debar Pertama* (1964); plays – *Di Mana Bulan Selalu Retak* (1965), *Ke Mana Terbangnya Si Burung Senja* (1966), and *Wira Bukit* (1986); novels – *Salina* (1961), *Bulan Tak Bermadu di Fatehpur Sikri* (1966), *Sungai Mengalir Lesu* (1967), *Di Hadapan Pulau* (1978), *Langit Petang* (1980), *Daerah Zeni* (1985), *Hujan Pagi* (1987) which has been translated into English as *The Morning Post* (1991); poems – *Daun Semalu Pucuk Paku* (1975) and *Balada Hilang Peta* (1990).

Wild in the Fire

I

Has it been three twilights now since my hands bled,
my beloved's hair fell, her breast throbbing
and, her eyes wilting, she asking:
for how many more days will the world burn?

I did not tremble hearing such news,
not surprised that my beloved's body was always cold
I handed her a purple letter
and said with dry lips: 'A letter without words'.

Several times have I unfolded the purple letter
coming from a secret country

7

several times have I read it, its meaning always eluding me
because the inscription was only a drop of blood.

For how many more days will my hands bleed
my beloved's hair fall, her breast be crushed
and her eyes become too blurred to ask:
in how many more days will we be destroyed?

I didn't know the answer; I held out my bleeding hands.
I looked at my beloved's face, I tried to explain:
ask the 'Sputnik' and 'Explorer' that crashed against my chest,
ask the 'Nautilus' and the satanic jets that penetrated my head
ask the five continents that have twice bled
whether they still have enough blood to drain into the third
river?

I saw my dear one's eyes shining, her wet lips
moving for a moment, smiling, then parting:
will we lose this fatherland?
I forced a smile at her and answered:
the purple letter has no meaning for me
being splattered with blood.

For how many twilights must my hands bleed
my beloved's hair fall, her breast throb
and her eyes droop, without questioning why
the world will burn.
'We die with the purple letter', she said sadly,
'the folly of one or two men'.

II

I see crossroads everywhere,
thinking for seven years to choose a path
to think for another seven
then to approach the brink of the last ravine:
where all of us fall
man and his fate
his hope and love,
hell and heaven,
wildly burning in the eternal fire.

Has it been three twilights now since my hands bled
the bitter poison has penetrated my breast!

(*translated by Muhammad Haji Salleh*)

Touch-Me-Nots

Leaves of touch-me-nots and fern shoots
tremble in the rain.

And in the young night
I hear the restless river;
as the dawn spreads out,
river and fish are calmed.

Leaves of touch-me-nots and fern shoots
my love blooms with you
even when I am more charmed by
the widow's wink on the verandah.

Leaves of forget-me-nots and fern shoots
I cannot forget.

(*translated by Muhammad Haji Salleh*)

On the Bunds

A quiet river beyond the fields
I stood beside it
watching a love-bird fly
overhead, faintly adorning the evening.

The mother has not returned, her daughter
remains on the bunds – with a lace blouse, wet sarong;
a brooch, a couple of rings –

refusing to move
unless the black snake's carcase is removed
from beside the wild
touch-me-nots, and unless
I go away.

For nine years I did not see
this beauty and this pity.
Now a young child, with a scar on its forehead,
runs, looks back, pulling
the girl's hand, pointing
to the quietly gliding love-birds
and the silent familiar evening.
Why must she look towards me, before she leaves
as if a promise had been broken and secrets still
abound?

(*translated by Muhammad Haji Salleh*)

Anxiety

Only fear becomes the fertile
season in the fields
rivers, rails, and the well washing area
and the prayer houses. And seeing
the surprises, panicky iguana becomes a huge net
tightening over the village.

For a week he recognised the nation's
face – in the critical places,
a fire; at the foothills,
poisonous; in the jungles,
full of thorns. The thrice-received
letter – broke our hearts.
Why, why did they let their son
go?

Only the worlds of their spirit hunt the fear –
over the rails they imagine their son running;
in the river they saw him wash; at the well
they pictured him standing; in the prayer house,
his image of loneliness. And though in the forest now,
with the twilight,
we saw him with a smile.

At that moment
a machine-gun barrel appeared
surprising their son,
suddenly frozen and riddled with bullets.

They cared for their son's favourite ferns
not knowing he shall not eat them.

(translated by Muhammad Haji Salleh)

Leaving

The kenanga flowers
that he sent, though
withered, were
on the table, enlivened
by the freshness
of her heart.

(In the room
alone she slept
the bliss of dream. But
waking up, she
shuddered; each dawn
forlorn).

The kenanga flowers,
sweet in her hand,
he left by the well.
He has

not returned since,
she wept
in the padi fields.

(*translated by Muhammad Haji Salleh*)

Under the Twinkling Stars

I
(letter from a waitress)

Under the twinkling stars I want to be alone
without books, without songs, without longing
but who can believe that the moon too can be grieving
while the world is passionately festive

Under the twinkling stars I want to be melancholic
without father without mother without my beloved
but who will believe that the night too can be grieving
while true lovers make love in damansara

Wild winds scatter the *kenanga* flowers
shaking my heart to its roots
therefore under the twinkling stars I sorrow
without lake, without memory, without anyone

Adam, if you have compassion
scatter my grave with flowers.

II
(letter to a waitress)

While the twilight reddened your fevered letter arrived
I read it with a throbbing heart
why, under the twinkling stars, must you suffer
speaking of the grave and flowers

Books, songs and longing – father, mother and beloved
into the lagoon of ours has sailed our story
but I still wander, not knowing which way I am driven
I cannot bear to see you sorrowing in the magnificence of
    evening

In the storm here the *kenanga* trees crashed to the ground
jolting my breast, rattling the pulses
but I cannot guess who will arrive first at the estuary
because we will leave this transit Island
Eve, if it is true that you sorrow
then half of it is already mine.

(translated by Muhammad Haji Salleh)

Thank You

Asleep with you, with your body exposed in the restive night,
I am part of your restlessness, that perhaps
grew from your dreams. Holding your hands, listening
to your quiet breath everything turns mysterious.
Once again returning almost nightly to all this
since the occupation of the Japanese, their surrender
and our independence
only this is happiness, only this is happiness.

Frequently with the quiet moon in the window,
rubber trees in the backyard, there's nothing that I wanted
but to squeeze your hands, and embrace
your exposed body. And in whispers saying:
I thank you, rubber tree, though dry of latex.
Thank you for making my life, though over-anxious
in the day, but ecstatic in the night.

(translated by Muhammad Haji Salleh)

A. WAHAB ALI

Born on 2 March 1941 in Selangor, A. Wahab Ali was once a teacher. He obtained his BA and MA (Literature) from the University of Malaya, Kuala Lumpur, and his PhD from the Australian National University. In 1977/78 he participated in the International Writing Programme at the University of Iowa in the USA. He is currently a Professor in the Department of Malay Studies, University of Malaya. He writes poetry, short stories, novels and essays. His published works are: novel – *Angin Hitam* (1968); poems – *Pemburu* (1968), *Penemuan* (1975), and *Sajak Orang Berdosa* (1977); and his thesis *Imej Manusia Dalam Sastera*. His poems won the Malaysian Literary Prize in 1985.

Existence

am i always
the loyal
tilted door
agreeing to
each man who enters
and submitting
to the man who exists?

i am like you, who,
once in a while
must lock up myself
to write:
      no

(*translated by Muhammad Haji Salleh*)

The Fallen Image

we meet,
in a room, most luxurious,
though no more than
in a zoo

you the warden with your charges
and i a visitor with my camera
those that i snapped
were your officers
each acting out gestures
from a show

the lasting thing
from the meeting
is only my memory
observing films
projecting
images of fallen beings.

(*translated by Muhammad Haji Salleh*)

Hello Death

a phone message for me time unknown
'call from your girl' i am disturbed
in longing there is no boundary to time its better
that way.

(*translated by Muhammad Haji Salleh*)

Whispers in Kuala Terengganu

am i a stranger
to a house once known,
or an in-law
with hands reached out
under a green blouse

it's as if my senses are lying
i am lost
tourism comes to
women in pants and blouse,
friends, ex-nationalist undergraduates
change cars and houses
entertaining new friends with the official stamp
or to the dot hotel for hot local girls
or perhaps it's better to go away
from the heat of old discussion

or am i an alien
hypnotized by stories
of taxi-drivers and frozen friends
who tell of starvation, of isolated families
arrests for thefts of tapioca in kuala brang
and sick old people from behind the hills in want of food
worrying over the freedom of their girls

is the university dead,
burying me under books
while over there life breeds like snakes
heads spinned by things material
women and development
forgiving oneself and situation
accepting it intellectually:
modernization is anti-tradition
and we build a selective morality

(*translated by Muhammad Haji Salleh*)

The Mountain Breaker

here is
a massive mountain.

here is a stone breaker
small and smart
versed in the dance of the hammer and tool
the psychology of the rock's density.

the rustling heat forgets the pounding on the rocks
the rain stops, entranced by the piercing chisel sound.

the massive mountain is flattened
on its site
stands the stone breaker
a general sings
watching the mountain range
life
prostrate and subjugated.

(translated by Muhammad Haji Salleh)

BAHA ZAIN

Baha Zain is the pen-name of Baharuddin Zainal. Born on 22 May 1939 in Perak, he received his education at the University of Malaya and the University of Indonesia. Baha Zain was formerly Head of the Literature Department and Deputy Director General of Dewan Bahasa dan Pustaka. Baha Zain received the SEA Write Award in Bangkok in 1980. His published poetry includes: *Perempuan dan Bayang-Bayang* (1974), *Dari Kertas Catatan Tengah Malam* (1978), and *Tiga Catatan Perjalanan* which has been translated into English as *Three Sketches From A Journey* (1980).

A 'Modern Movement' Collage

petrol fumes, tractor smoke
flats, massage parlours
women & hotel = prostitute
mascara, eye-shadow = floor show
(Beware of Dogs) bungalow
aquarium & orchid, poodle & piano
antique chairs, classical music
status + symbol = modern − progressive
'cheap sale' at the new supermarket

invitation card
reception
R.S.V.P.
tel: 8891
lounge suit
cocktails
b.g. ale
whisky soda
et cetera

in a city lane
the artist asks for directions
looking for a gallery
to exhibit his collage
a collector
purchases his painting
and in the grand hall
hangs a false collage.

(*translated by Muhammad Haji Salleh*)

Plea of the Asian Woman

what else can I give
all frangipanis wilt in the fire of the blasts
you have filled all wombs
with your dollars
with your V.D.

what else
what else
you have left me
heir to diseases and destruction
let me be

the prostitute at the hotel embassy
she cries,
'Hei, Jo, gip me yor dolar
not your napam, not yor gonoria.'

(*translated by Muhammad Haji Salleh*)

Toilet Paper City

the city's feet are the wilderness
its nerves barbed wires
old, rusty and infected with tetanus
that bite into movement and vision
in the smoke of dust and soot
shattering the clarity
of ph.d minds, talents and personalities
become victims in the day's tangle
the repetition of life's routine
the white morning to wake up in
then to prostrate before a dark poisonous night.

this city is a den for grand planners
each to his own lot and direction
programming precise steps
adding – multiplying numbers on a bank card
analysing telex news of coup d'etat
libel suits of politicians against editors
tracker dogs from a news office
morphine pushers in the coffee house
and everyone recognises the sweet smile of the beer waitress
the receptionist, dancer and florist
as temporary cures
for all that irritates
and hastens anger.

the city is hard rocks
transforming into a region of conflict
the meeting of trouble shooters
student leaders, labourers, administrators and academicians
bricks to the city's rise
however hopeless the situation
we may not escape from ourselves
that together carry the burden and hate this filthy city
that emerges as cancer to environment's greenness

we cannot avoid boredom
because it gives us breath for another day

so what then must I do?
collect the tissue paper discarded by nose-wipers
manufactured from a hundred-year-old trees
or write poems on them
as the last notes
that may be reached by rubbish collectors:
this is paper from toilets
from a tissue-paper civilization
I seek for an answer
perhaps it's best that I resign tomorrow
and not report to the employment office
apply for a job at a big hotel
because the best and lucrative profession
is prostitution

(*translated by Muhammad Haji Salleh*)

Woman

your hair, the deep green jungle
your breath, the swift mountain gale
your love, the surf on the shore
and your passion, the wild tempests

my deep green jungle
my mountain gale
my surf on the shore
my wild tempests
tempt me with an ambiguous language
fire, wind, earth and water are words that compel
as if your violent desire reigns everywhere

then again I do not know you
waves of passion rage in your belly
hot breath scapes your lips
all these are beyond me
how terrifying the energy that moves
     beneath your skin

between the strands of your hair in your veins,
    in your subconscious
and between your feminine patience
    and wild desire

my woman, you who are created from smoke, steam, mist and
                      cloud
how thick is the night silk that wraps all dreams
how far the distance between myself and your secret
like a flourishing green jungle
impenetrable to light

like the scent of falling leaves
filling my lungs and breath
like the smell of a baby suckling at your breast
boundless joy
boundless danger
woman, I'll ride you on to the wide open fields
your voice echoes into the unknown like the neighing of a
                      horse
swallowed by stillness but the dust at your feet blurs the scene
you gallop on ceaselessly from one field to another
no one ever knowing the colour of the hair that wraps your
                      body.

(*translated by Muhammad Haji Salleh*)

A Child's Sketch

I

sun,
I place you on the horizon,
moon,
I put you between the trees' crown and the clouds
may you rest there
and not have to climb higher
I love to see you from this window.

II

sun,
tomorrow I shall colour you green,
but moon,
if it rains tomorrow night
I shall reserve you the black
because you are not gay
and I am eternally sad

III

I cannot again
place you as my heart desires
over the bamboo leaves, beside clouds, at the horizon,
I must leave you
to rise
whether you are black or green
and I myself am
far away
in your shadows.

(*translated by Muhammad Haji Salleh*)

Postponing Truth

I lie naked in bed
facing the lonely mirror
my body suffers, my skin pales
like a century's pain collected in a single moment
inviting destruction yet postponing it
indefinitely

my love, fresh and desiring
I have lied to you under the pregnant moonlight
in the quietness that needs no speech
under the shelter of a temporary truth
and now the eyes that I see in the mirror torture me
because I can no longer belong to them

I should be among friends
or talking to diplomats, professors or lawyers
all of them have the same inclination
lying to their women, children and friends
I should not be writing poetry again
it's better to wander the dark lanes
or just lie on the breast of their inhabitants
because for them all lies and promises
never come true.

(*translated by Muhammad Haji Salleh*)

Those Pills from the Family Planning Clinic

I took a long look at my wife
yes, she is like a maiden
and I am submerged in boredom
so I cast a dream
into her womb,
nothing unusual, is it?
a year later
she only imagined it
but could not deliver.

those pills from the family planning clinic
impregnate women in the heads
and make men meaningless riders.

(*translated by Muhammad Haji Salleh*)

Some Notes from the Past

i

what's left are
scattered stars
sad christmas trees
and in their midst
a girl
kneeling before a cross
praying for patience

what's remembered
are happenings
that come like dreams
eclipsed by daylight
they torment in the night
my suffering is the world's
unceasing
I watch a girl
kneeling before a cross
her figure silhouetted
against the harbour's edge
praying for peace
never weary

ii

when the windows are opened
the breeze blows in from the bay
and light colours the trees
casting their shadows on green grass
together with the silence
the breeze that plays over my face
has paused over seas, mountains, gardens and over my
                                          beloved's room
carrying sweet news of the woman in bed
filled with longing and love without bounds
gazing into her cheeks, lips and dark eyes in the mirror
as she pins a white flower to her hair
and builds her hopes in the morning dream
only the breeze knows all is lost

between the waiting girl and the lover is a space that must
                                                    be filled
with corals, fishes, fresh water and green plants,
passions that torment all
that will compel us to finally cry out:
'may this mysterious meeting
transmute into a dream
in the tight clench of night and day
until all memories fade away.'

                              iii
perhaps I shall never possess your heart
except in dreams
but whatever grows from this poem
is my love.

                              iv
suddenly the purple chrysanthemum wilts
its petals scattered on the table
like a season coming to an end
like a storm dying to a calm
all is cold.

am I as I was
as loving tender and easily yearning
is everything to remain unanswered
about the darkening shadows within me?

(*translated by Muhammad Haji Salleh*)

Dharmawijaya

Dharmawijaya is the pen-name of Kamaruzzaman Abdul
Kadir. Born in Negeri Sembilan on 23 June 1937,
Dharmawijaya was once a teacher and is now an
Associate Professor at the University of Malaya, from
which he received his BA and MA. Among his works are
Warna Maya (1975) and several books on the study of
poetry. A number of his essays and poems have won the
Malaysian Literary Prize.

My Village

the fountain of my love, my village
how have you fared
laterite roads,
hennaed with dust
its fields and swamps
in drought, often.

the land of longing, my village
your children
are grown and adult
patiently begging
in the jaws of sorrow
and its festival
bathing the sunshine
adrift alone.

my village
in the soul of your children
waiting in anxiety
for the world's abundance
will be consumed by silence
and its belief

yes, fills its chest
and prayers sad

my village
has understood
that its children's happiness
is merely
counting stars
in the bright moonlight.

(translated by Muhammad Haji Salleh)

Colours of Illusion

sorrow is
    a honeycomb
    human children
    with ambition of iron

happiness is
    a breeze of dust
    human children
    addicts of girls

sorrow-happiness
    is the colour of illusion
    its shores and seas
    its chest

        the journey!

(translated by Muhammad Haji Salleh)

There Still Exists

twitter of birds upon tips of twigs still exist
their morning wings deprived of wind
while daylight waves on
flies home.

a seaman flops upon the lips of a beach where still exists
his breast of twilight shoves back waves
while night draws nigh
to fence in dreams.

birds and seaman
here
their hearts exchange greetings
before they depart to bear their pain
to other ports.

(translated by Barclay M. Newman)

The Eternal Peasant

if you inquire
about the house of life
that gives rest to fatigue
I shall answer
its night and day
are like the rain and storm
planting stakes into the spread
of the padi fields.

if you inquire
about the room of tranquility
that lulls anxiety
I shall answer
its calmness
is like the call of the drought

blowing waves into the young padi
all chaff.

if you inquire
about the brilliance of hope
I shall reply
you are the eternal peasant
absorbing the pale of the moon
mopping the clouds of the sun
beating out governance
on the tongue of fate.

(*translated by Muhammad Haji Salleh*)

FIRDAUS ABDULLAH

Firdaus Abdullah was born on 3 June 1944 in Selangor. He received his secondary education in Kuala Lumpur. He was a journalist with the newspaper *Berita Harian* before he continued his studies in political science at the University of Northern Illinois in the USA (1966–67). He obtained his masters degree from the University of Ohio and, in 1980, his PhD from Columbia University, New York. His collections of poems are *Balada Cinta di Seberang Benua* (1976) and *Prisma Mimpi* (1985). Several of his poems have won the Malaysian Literary Prize. Firdaus has translated a number of foreign books on literature and political science into Malay. He is currently a lecturer in the faculty of Economics and Administration, University of Malaya, Kuala Lumpur.

Song for Sariyati

cold winds
and wet snow
damp shoes
and unfinished tasks
but I must be patient
but I must be patient

flakes float
beyond the windows
I am shut up
in a seminar room
where are you, sariyati
I am a storyteller without an audience

a dry hamburger
and an unwilling appetite
the path of fate

31

and surrender
rather than allow sariyati to suffer
let her not understand

if sariyati were here
I should warmly embrace
your whole body
till the white snow
and seminar room
become a volcano in the morning
like mount singkaran lighted by the sun.

(*translated by Muhammad Haji Salleh*)

Waiting for One Who Waits

Everything is here
        poetry and music
        flutes and ballads
all I need is you
        wise and clever
        dressed in your white prayer-veil

Everything waits outside
        flickering neon lights
        and dark temptations
all they need is me
        late and lost
        caught in sin.

(*translated by Muhammad Haji Salleh*)

Return to Me

a pair of ears
with a sensitivity of old
to listen to the world's noise
nodding in its silence

return to me
a pair of eyes
with a sharpness of old
to see all that is buried between the lines
to observe and appreciate

return to me
the heart beat and the pulse
as of old
with the tear ducts
that are ready to cry
and the well of laughter with a pail of belief
to feel and to wisely anticipate

bestow upon me
the essence
lips and tongue
that know no silence and no fatigue
graceful in its loving caress
agile and ready before reality.

(translated by Muhammad Haji Salleh)

Five Thoughts at Five Stops

subang:
how clear
the tears
on every cheek
i love.
but who

can guess
that each tear
contains a mystery
unlike the other

karachi:
i remember it all
the last few weeks
in kuala lumpur
poison and antidote
mixed thick in a glass.

house of Allah:
give me wisdom
especially

house of Allah:
o Allah, omniscient Allah
give me wisdom
especially
to make a decision

o Allah, omnipotent Allah
give me
boldness
and strength
especially
to do what i decide

o merciful one
give me
mercy and happiness
the outcome
of every decision.

o parents
whom i love
who pray with me
at the kaaba
accompany all
with your prayers.

beirut:
how luxurious
how robust
'phoenicia inter-continental hotel'
just like
a haughty smile
it sees my desire
to weep
while tears won't flow from my eyes.

new york:
i come to you
a poet
without words
instruct me
to be crude

new york
instruct me
to be a man
of wisdom

(*translated by Barclay M. Newman*)

KASSIM AHMAD

Kassim was born in Kedah on 9 September 1933. He
joined the University of Malaya (Singapore) in 1955,
graduated with a BA in 1959, and an MA in 1961. He
worked with Dewan Bahasa dan Pustaka as research
officer from June 1960 until 31 October 1962. From
November 1962 to February 1966, Kassim was a lecturer
at the London School of Oriental and African Studies in
London, before resigning and devoting his time to
Malaysian politics. Currently, he devotes most of his
time to writing and translation. Among his published
literary works are: *Kemarau di Lembah* (anthology of
short stories and poems, 1967), *The Characterisation in
Hikayat Hang Tuah* (1964), *Dialog Dengan Sasterawan*
(1979) and *Risalah Seni Karang Mengarang* (1979).

Dialogue
(for my mother)

I

be calm now my son
though our field is flooded
this rain is from God
who pours down his blessings.

day will come, shall it not be bright
listen
the frogs have stopped calling
tomorrow will be a bright day
our padi will ripen!

II

go to sleep now, mother
we are frail beings
struggling through the days
and worrying the nights

there is the day, there must be sun
I will go
with a thousand Jebats of the peasantry
we have long died in loyalty
now will live in defiance!

(*translated by Muhammad Haji Salleh*)

Your Poet

of your poet
you demand
songs from a serene heart
in harmony with the world.

my poet –
his hut by the stream
his heart embracing the wide world
meditates upon his situation.

he says
I have lost my peace
and you are the hunter
I shall never return

he says
I consider my children born in sin
guaranteed of hunger
I confront this reality.

your poet –
his heart is bleeding
your ambition is to purchase beauty
listen to the song you play.

(*translated by Muhammad Haji Salleh*)

Wanderer's Journey

I

ah, time!
how the years pass away
north, south, east, west
I postpone all questions
and neglect the demands of ambition.

dear inspiration!
where have
the sun, skies, oceans and mountains
the moon, night and man gone to?
you are so cold to beauty!

no! a call from
another world:
pain and suffering
ignorance, hunger and colonialism;
man and earth shaken by waves and storms.

the rise of man
from man's oppression
wars, rebellions, revolutions
actions and reactions
from loss of harmony.

II

dear traveller!
– we are all in the midst of the journey
seeking the road home
in the vast universe without
skies, oceans, mountains and jungles.

man emerged from the earth's womb
the sun, oceans, mountains, trees and animals
are bound by a code of laws;
except their freedom
to obey or rebel.

the universe has its ways
a traveller
among countless others
a straight road
among diversions
for the return journey.

poor mankind!
seven thousand years of civilization
from a naked hunter of animals
to a builder of cities
with factories, plantations, banks, universities and parliaments
your eyes see distant stars
your ships sail the waves, colonise space
a salute to man
how great his achievements!

III
standing proud on his summit of power
free, independent, conceited and arrogant
I am man, great and sovereign
with the sciences, the bombs and machines
I will conquer the world and the universe.

IV
ah, forgetful man!
can you conquer the world
without conquering yourself?
the pharoah, napoleon, hitler, tojo, mussolini
the empires of persia, rome, portugal, holland, britain, japan
emerged and exited on history's stage,
witness your own pettiness.

look around you!
starvation, poverty and diseases
colonialism and oppression
man driven out of his homeland
children, women and the old burnt alive –
wars, murders and disputes
are your life's environment.

ah, man
how great your achievements
but yet how great also
your failures!

V

a traveller amidst his journey
finding the road home
pausing for a moment of meditation
purifies his soul from conceit
to receive knowledge.

because eyes are blind
if they do not see
ears are deaf
if they hear without comprehension;
because of their own denial.

I am a traveller
on the road home
like the sun, mountains, oceans, trees and animals
choosing the straight road
among diversions
to return home.

(*translated by Muhammad Haji Salleh*)

A Pact
(*for the forgotten heroes of the land*)

those who are my brothers, come
I don't care who you are
we have a pact to make
against the enemies of our land

Admiral Cheng-Ho has returned
with his truth, we don't care if not in strength

Rama is safe with Sita
his golden bow is strung.

Then let Tuah rise and speak
whether of God or *jin*
whatever our colour or blood
whatever our race
we are born men.

Those who are my brothers, step forward
I don't care for style and parliament
we shall make a pact here in blood
against all the enemies of mankind.

together, together let us march, my brothers
like Tuah and Jebat of old
we have named our sacred land
we ourselves will guard her shores
come then, you busy policemen of the world!

(*translated by Kassim Ahmad*)

Assembly of Souls

I

there is a need to reassess one by one
now that we are mature
without god without dreams
because tomorrow may be too late
for the judgement that was postponed.

i am no cynic
call me no atheist
my speech is from those who have forgotten how to live
the words are necessary
lest we die from loss of speech.

if you believe in man in the state of peace
do not celebrate to rules
(your victory)
if you believe in the free man
do not take to law
(your loyalty)
because there is no legitimate law
(though it is enacted in the u.n.)
that has no constitution in the heart.

II

the most cruel news has arrived
for those who still live because they still hope:
this world is a prison
our rice shall be sufficient in paradise.
we have traded this life
on the Devil's back
the laughter and the sneakers giggles are not of happiness
they are the laughter and giggles of the destitute.

all souls will assemble to discuss
what your children eat today
rice or beer
the laughter is false, the cries voiceless.

III

the torch from the high minaret
shall die by itself
because man is progressively drunk
and God is dead.

(*translated by Muhammad Haji Salleh*)

KEMALA

Kemala (Ahmad Kamal Abdullah) was born in Selangor on 30 January 1941. While working as a teacher, he first tried his hand at writing poems, short stories, dramas and essays on literature. He obtained his BA and MA (Literature) from the Science University of Malaysia in 1980 and 1985, respectively. He is now Head of the Modern Literature Unit, Dewan Bahasa dan Pustaka Malaysia. He has published several anthologies of poetry, such as *Meditasi* (1972), *Timbang Terima* (1973), *Era* (1975), *Kaktus-kaktus* (1976), *Ayn* (1983), *Meditation and Other Poems* (1986), and *Pelabuhan Putih* (1989). He was awarded the SEA Write Award in Bangkok in 1986. Recently, Kemala has ventured his creative talent into painting and held his first exhibition in Kuala Lumpur in early February 1992.

Ocean

I'm the ocean
a lovely maiden asleep on her royal bed
the scales of ripple over my body
a moment's sketch and dancing winds
unite and hiss with desire
for this calm expanse

I'm the ocean
an agile youth nurtured by time
the foam of waves become words
a roar that reaches toward the horizon
its music is stranded on coral dikes
then knows itself.

choice daylight
binds together quatrains of seagulls
history passes on

43

I carry your language
I, the primeval ocean,
creator of eternal love

night's gamble
courageous hurricanes embrace my presence
enigma and supreme mystery
radiated by the one who discovered meaning
for space and time
I'm the ocean, possessor of song

grandmother's affection, grandchild's mischief
meet here
distant winds seek harmony
lips quiver in commentary
here: in this heart of my beloved
boils self-esteem.

(*translated by Barclay M. Newman*)

See

see my fingers form small trees
see my hands become branches pointing the way
see my feet form a bridge across a stream
see my ears are shady groves of bamboo
see my hair is a clump of cactus thorns
see my eyes shine with the gentle light of day
see my tongue tells of love's first blossom
see my neck turns to the cry of the heron
see my adam's apple moves to the taste of mountain water
see my heart beats at the mention of your name
see my soul shines like a pearl in a golden chalice
see My Self hidden in Your Self.

(*translated by Harry Aveling*)

In the Distance

bring yourself
to the snow-field
and personality
to the deep jungle
shrill barkings of night-dogs
fall steeply into the emptiness of dawn
where is the final edge
of pure forgiveness?

in the distance.

eva was ignorant of sin
deceived by temptation
paradise was under trial
everlasting pleasure
making her uncomfortable & sick
eva wanted maturity
escaping from
adam's captivity.

and as for adam
separation wasn't a caltrop
but nectar
pleasure wasn't a green image
but a yearning
that flew through the sky
sprouting on the earth
left alone and isolated

in the distance.

in the snow-field
molecules were more beautiful
serenity was the beginning of life
self. a flower of negligence
ousted from god's paradise
eva searching her own way.

in the distance.

(*translated by Ahmad Kamal Abdullah*)

That Love, My Beloved

that love my beloved, is myself
the part of a goblet that's full
a day at fusion of dawn, morning, dusk & night
all gathered in one sacred word: worship
i live not by understanding all mankind
my life's the billows and wanderings of my poetry

leaves at year's end fall from old trees
a parable coils about pain and joy of past times
that life, a life sadness & happiness
no greetings for it, greetings are for
the universe and God, from him all alone we
have sipped lovely honey and its pleasure the ultimate love

that love my beloved, is gathered in meditation
it brings us together, did you realize this?
a strange and miraculous power which cannot be defeated by
                                                              deeds

of men and machines, we are self and ourselves
for this, for love we live and become its friends
and pass along on the strength and will of his love.

(*translated by Barclay M. Newman*)

Quatrain of January

(a)
Noah calls me in this dawn with flood
My ark is on the mountain's wing
My followers are on the palm of wind
Do embrace them wholeheartedly this morning.

(b)
I engraved your name, freely my love
The streets are quiet and empty
I engraved your name, freely my love
But just the nun came with roses of love.

(c)
This milk is for the innocent ones
Let Mama and Papa say grace
Just this moment breaks the silence
And gone is my long sleepy night.

(d)
For Noah is my big thank you
That is echoing your love, O Allah
My love is tenderly exposed
And also there are tears of melancholy.

(*translated by Ahmad Kamal Abdullah*)

December ii

the soul's tree
decorates south sky

and this life
exhausts in peace

are you the one who
cries towards fate

and humanity
on the lips of angels' war

this red rose, love
in my breast forever

(*translated by Ahmad Kamal Abdullah*)

The Room

For what purpose you are numbered
while we
can see every daily happening
from the left, middle or right room
herewith the sharp wind's song
slicing us
one very dimension
yes, once more
for what purpose you are numbered?

(*translated by Ahmad Kamal Abdullah*)

Coral

I know coral
coral stretching in endless reefs
I know coral
spiky and sharp
like a shining knife
or the blade of a sword
stabbing the gentle breast of a mermaid
the soft flesh of a dugong
when, when the storm starts
the storm, when . . . when

the tornado descends
nature's destructive order
it covers the sailor's troubled dream
with flowers of fire
it drowns the pearl-diver's delight
a lamp flickers on the beach
but he cannot come home
there is no trace of where he has been
no sign of love's bloodless wounds
only eyes and ribs
only tongue and lips
screaming as the surf wildly pounds
against the coral
a symphony searching
the face of the old musician
in love with the poetry of the heavens
while the earth whispers
although there is no one to translate
the weeping of the waves
and the raging of the storm
I know coral
coral contained
within myself
I know coral
coral in the paths of poetry
no one mourns
the white seagull in my body
the warm blood
dripping from its throat

Kuala Lumpur
1980

(*translated by Harry Aveling*)

LATIFF MOHIDIN

Born on 25 August 1941 in Negri Sembilan, Latiff
Mohidin was educated at Lenggeng, Seremban, Singapore, and the University of Fine Arts in Berlin. This poet
and artist has held exhibitions of his works and travelled
abroad extensively in the 1960s and 1970s. He has served
as Writer in Residence at the Science University of
Malaysia, Penang, the National University of Malaysia
and Dewan Bahasa dan Pustaka. At present, Latiff is a
freelance poet and artist. His poems have won the
Malaysia Literary Prize many times and his collection
Pesisir Waktu (1980) won the Putra I Poetry Award.
Among his books are: *Sungai Mekong* (1972), *Kembara
Malam* (1974), and *Wayang Pak Dalang* (1977). *Garis:
Dari Titik ke Titik* (1988), a book on the creative process
(art and poetry), won the Honourable Diploma Prize at
the Festival of International Books at Leipzig, Germany
in 1989.

Dream I

one night
all the inhabitants
within a stone fort
received an identical
dream.

they dreamt
that on the morrow
they would walk
around the fort, the day long
regularly spaced
their shoulders carrying a slab of stone
of identical shape
never tiring
never thirsting

on the morrow
the dream became real
silent and without appetite
they were quite happy
though they did not understand
how such a thing
could happen.

(*translated by Muhammad Haji Salleh*)

Mirror

I look out of the window
and see myself
walking to and fro
in the yard
shoulder a mirror

it is late night
I inspect my palms
reopen their dressing
there's no line of cut
when i close the window
I hear a mirror breaking
on the steps

(*translated by Muhammad Haji Salleh*)

The Puppeteer's Wayang

the wayang is over
rawana is dead
no longer the curses and blood
no longer bitterness and lightning
the skies are again at peace

for the hundredth time
rama and sita
live happily
in the chest

now,
puppeteer
you may sleep soundly
on the shredded
banana trunk

but look
puppeteer,
the audience is still standing
still standing
waiting
for rawana to return to life
waiting
for the wayang to begin once more

(*translated by Muhammad Haji Salleh*)

Words Adrift on Air

over my eyebrows the fields of moss are silent
over my breastwater caterpillars are still

slowly, trees drift down to the estuary
cold winds creep uphill

I recall dawn poems
thinning and hushed rows of words

words adrift on air
their shadows frozen on the lake's bed

the dark night is encircled with translucence
the thick and hard face of a mirror

the light of your pen flashes in a single moment
with words, seemingly vocal

(translated by Muhammad Haji Salleh)

The Legend of the Dawn

death arrives quietly in the dawn
softly knocking on the gates of the city
its keeper an ancient evasive man
smiles respectfully while arranging his words:

I welcome your presence noble sirs
as I have in the past years and centuries
especially in these early hours
truly you need have no doubt over the situation
witness the buildings roads hall and houses
all in quiet peaceful and each of its inhabitants
has long closed his eyes that are cold and
heavy as rocks on the walls of the gate
and brilliant lights
shine on numbers on the graves
in truth I am always aware of your presence
as you can witness now on these sign boards
isn't 'dead end' clearly visible there?

(translated by Muhammad Haji Salleh)

A City, A Grandmother and Death

then you come
to me, by the wayside
fathoming the flash of my eyes
my eyes; heavy pebbles
now, without lustre

do not hold out
your cold hands to me
let me cross
the silence of the city
alone, as always

I know
before us is
the cemetery of vehicles
dark metal slabs
that no longer terrify
after a thousand bends of their journey

let me walk on
without your magic words
in a moment will be the end
you will know too
something will happen here
in a flash and is then forgotten

(translated by Muhammad Haji Salleh)

His Thick Shroud

one day
after half a century
Truth
emerge once again
in the midst of a market place
unwrapping his shroud
piece by piece.

seeing that he was totally naked
people began to laugh
thinking that he was a crazy old man
one or two spat and cursed
others went on
with their own business.

unfortunately
no one
recognised him
Truth then wrapped himself up again
in his thick shroud
piece by piece
before disappearing
for another half a century.

(*translated by Muhammad Haji Salleh*)

The Shore of Time

it's an eternal battle between
the frozen and the fluid

the banks are raised higher
consequent waves bounce wilder

caught in the net of winds
rolling dazed before being jerked

thus the ebbing step begins
the idol crumbled, flat under feet

hypnotised by the strangeness of the sea's breast
we are tested by proverbs and the sun

(*translated by Muhammad Haji Salleh*)

Mask or My Name is Rawana

and we live happily until
the night of the eclipse of the moon i: seri rama
    released myself

from sita dewi's embrace in the palace of the fairy
    land and descended to earth
momentarily noticing layers of rawana's masks, crushed,
one by one, until I discovered my own face
eternally smiling there as though looking into the depth
of a mirror.

(*translated by Muhammad Haji Salleh*)

LIM SWEE TIN

Born on 26 September 1952 in Kelantan, Lim Swee Tin received his secondary education in Kelantan. He was a teacher before he joined the Agricultural University of Malaysia in Serdang and obtained his BA (Education). He is at present teaching in a school in Selangor. His poetry and short stories have time and again won prizes, including the Malaysia Literary Prize and the ESSO–GAPENA Short Stories Contest. His collections of poems are *Akrab*, *Eva*, and *Menyusur Musim*.

A Flute and That Old Man

I returned
to the almost deserted
verandah
a single flute
still hangs on the wall
here too
a well-trodden mat is still spread out.

the play and the dance
are already ancient
the legend and the story
have become old
in every corner
only the spiders
and their webs.

the stage and the theatre
are empty
where are
the ladies-in-waiting and the knights
only your flute

still hangs on the wall
there too
a well-trodden mat is spread out
where is the old man.

(translated by Muhammad Haji Salleh)

Mirror I

it has never
returned us our whole face °
under its translucent surface

truth before the mirror is a shadow
we, the cowards, are crafty fabricators of evidence.

(translated by Muhammad Haji Salleh)

Portrait of the xxth Century

when Hiroshima fell
disembowelled, puss splattered
on the ground and all around
from the eye of Nagasaki's breast the stench of puss
attacked human senses. not far
away are the bloody children's faces
and old mothers of Sabra-Chatilla
the hatred of tired Afghan fighters
and love is beheaded, shredded
everywhere skin colour becomes boundary
how distant is human love.

nothing can
soften our hearts,
is this how your map should be drawn
smeared with fire, your citizens blundering towards?

(translated by Muhammad Haji Salleh)

Remembering

the dry flowers in the vase
often remind me
and its hundred years

petals of memories
will never bloom,
yet their fragrance floats between us.

(translated by Muhammad Haji Salleh)

Pearl Poem

the blue sea, the beautiful world
and you who arrange in the quietness of my adulthood

this is an event of fascination and magic
as promised and planned

the moment of departure
fulfils my life, beyond it I decorate a woman's breast.

(translated by Muhammad Haji Salleh)

MOECHTAR AWANG

Born in Kelantan on 19 February 1956, Moechtar Awang received his early education in Kota Bharu before participating in the Descriptive and Creative Writing Programme, University of Malaya, where he obtained his BA in 1986. His collection of poems *Pasrah* (1981) won the Putra I Poetry Award. His second collection of poems *Qaf* was published in 1986. He is currently teaching at a secondary school in Kelantan.

Surrender I

a clot of silence
a quiver in the bowels of the night
suddenly falls on to a mirror
sprinkling the fragrance of fragipani
to the earth around mother's cemetery
my hands the soft silk
as though arranging velvet
reaching for Your heaven
that hushes all secrets
suddenly
my odorous and dirty face
kneels
at the doors Your ears
then to say a million prayers
prayers of purity from sin
prayers of freedom from revenge
prayers full of regret
prayers that request a million
forgivenesses.

(*translated by Muhammad Haji Salleh*)

Tok Bageh

prepare me
tumeric rice
from a million fields
betel-nut leaves
from a million plants
prepare me
the fragrance of incense
from every corner
well water
from a million districts
prepare me
farm eggs
prepare me
copper needles
prepare me
young coconuts
prepare me
seven bowls of dew
I will rise
with the soul of the earth
I will run
with the soul of the lightning
I will shout
with the soul of the thunder
I am the guardian
of all forests
I am the healer
of all diseases
I come
from the blue skies
with a noose on my neck
I jump from the peak of the hill
with a rope around my waist
I crawl
from between the flames
with chains on my feet
prepare me
drums big and small

their skin burnt by lightning
prepare me the violin and the lute
its strings and bow
blessed by a thousand saints
I shall take away
all diseases all lameness
by the favour
of our king
the prophet muhammad
I shall return
all health to bodies
I shall dissolve
each tension in the muscle
with the divine wish
of our God
ALLAH.

(*translated by Muhammad Haji Salleh*)

Incantation of Origins

a lump of earth
a drop of mud
a skeleton of bones
a lump of flesh
a string of blood
a piece of leather
a twinkle of light

puuhh!!!

you are free but not on the loose
you are together but not united
you are with face but not identical
puuhh!!!

return to the original seed of germination
return to the original place of departure

return to the original roots that erected you
return to the original rope that you held on to
return to the original step that you first took
return to the original sentence that began words
return to the original voice that is the source of oath
return to the original utterance that began promises
return to the beginning of the origins of movement
return to the step that begins the tread

puuhh!!!
you chisel at your own existence.

(*translated by Muhammad Haji Salleh*)

Season of Sorrow

i
the drought has perched
on the fields
the straw burst into fire
the moment has alighted
on the sea
fishes aflapping

ii
my peasant
there is a smell of drought
in your rice vase
    sorrow has perched
    on your children's eyes
my sailor
there is a howl of the waves
in your pots and pans
    laughter has turned to silence
    on your wife's breast.

(*translated by Muhammad Haji Salleh*)

A Message to a Wife (II) (for AS)

(your tongue
is a snake
wound around
your mouth
that strikes at
your own body)

speak with Mary's tongue
she who brought us together
from the garden of eden
as the waters of the cool mountain
at the end of my feet
gentle and translucent
speak in the language of Masyitath
that curls around your soul's mist
like the voice of your Angel
bringing the command to read
gentle and translucent
gentle and translucent
then to reside
in my breast
your husband.

(*translated by Muhammad Haji Salleh*)

Muhammad Haji Salleh

Born on 26 March 1942 in Taiping, Perak Muhammad Haji Salleh received his education at the High School Bukit Mertajam; the Malay College Kuala Kangsar; Malayan Teachers Training College, Brinsford Lodge, UK; the University of Malaya; and the University of Michigan, where he obtained his PhD. He currently holds the post of Professor at the National University of Malaysia. In 1991 Muhammad was awarded the sixth Malaysian National Literary Award. He has also received the ASEAN Write Award (for poetry) at Bangkok in 1977. His poetry books are: *Sajak-sajak Pendatang* (1973), *Buku Perjalanan Si Tenggang II* (1975), translated as *The Travel Journals of Si Tenggang* (1979), *Ini Juga Duniaku* (1977), translated as *Time and Its People* (1978), *Sajak-sajak Sejarah Melayu* (1981), *Kalau, Atau dan Maka* (1988), and, as editor, *An Anthology of Contemporary Malaysian Literature* (1988).

Si Tenggang's Homecoming

i

the physical distance that i traverse
is a journey of the soul,
transport of the self from a fatherland
to a country collected by sight and mind,
the knowledge that sweats from it
is a stranger's knowledge,
one who has learnt to see, think
and choose between
changing realities.

ii

it is true i have spoken in anger at my mother and grandmother,
but only after having told them of my predicament
that they have never brought to understanding.

the wife that i began to love in my loneliness,
in the country that alienated me,
they took to their prejudices.
i am no longer afraid of oceans
having been changed by time and place,
coarsened by problems
estranged by absence.

                                    iii

but look,
i have brought myself home,
seasoned with self-assurance,
broadened by land and languages,
i am no longer afraid of the oceans
or the difference between people,
not easily confused
by words or ideas.
the journey was a loyal teacher
who was never tardy
in explaining cultures or differences.
look i am just like you
still malay,
sensitive to what
i believe is good,
and more ready to understand
than my brothers.
the contents of this ship are yours too
because i have returned.

                                    iv

travel made me
a seeker who does not take
what is given without sincerity
nor entertain demands of payments from my beliefs.
the years at sea and in coastal states
have taught me to choose,
to accept only those tested by comparison,
or that which accords with the words of my ancestors,
that which returns me to my village
and its verities.

v

I have learnt
to be raw,
to hold reality in a new logic
debate with hard and clear facts.
but
I am humble too, respecting
man and life.

vi

i am not a new man,
not too different
from you;
the people and cities
of coastal ports
taught me not to brood,
over a foreign world
suffer difficulties
or fear possibilities.

i am you,
freed from the village,
its soil and ways,
independent, because
i have found myself.

(translated by Muhammad Haji Salleh)

Prologue

'We have heard that there is a Malay history brought from
Goa let's improve it with due ceremony so that our
descendants may learn from it, and remember it and
consequently gain benefit therefrom.'

revered prime minister, tun mamat
write us our history,
of the malays and all their islands,

return us to the soaring siguntang
to samudera, across the waters,
to the javanese in the southeast, the buginese in the sea's
                                                    abdomen.
to the people in the fields, forests and on the beaches.

you are the bard,
great is your role, all must be given their due
language and the turn of time,
the might of nations and the conscience of man,
but of the greatest importance
because truth is the matter of history
critic of kings and reminder of the forgetful,
the impartial pointer
that will not break under blows.

please write a history for those who come after us
describe for them how we live in our times
and how our forefathers
ruled over the land and tilled it.

tell all,
so that they may be proud with their pride,
paint the forts and jetties, the orchards and ports
forests of the mountains, rivers of the valleys
with your ink,
give colour to good and evil,
the pure and wicked heart
draw out the nerves of time,
swing them to the top of the page
when we were a great empire and have self-knowledge,
let it loose when we surrendered
and forget the meaning of pride.

fill the straits with water,
that cleansed the boundaries of the state,
give homage to the seas
that have brought us here,
opening and populating the bazaars,
drawing junks and barges from china,

making space for the indians and their cloth,
and the portuguese in awe of malacca's ways.

appraise its people,
rajas in the palaces
the prime ministers and their wisdom,
the brave and loyal retainers,
wars fought on the waters,
or on the shores of the oceans,
paint the beauty of malay princesses
with the gentle nuances of your words
for there was none to compare with them.

speak of the justice
of the rajas, princes and ministers
show with the evidence of history
how dignity and majesty
grow from the nurture of equality,
and the waters polluted by slander,
or made turbid by shadows
of kings and ministers
who stand before mirrors
will kill all,
rot the palace floors,
break the throne's pillars
and flow into the people's well,
in the city or distant villages.

and revered prime minister, forget not
the reflection of gold that often glints
in the lords' eyes
and their officers in the hall,
with all your talent,
paint a picture of how power is mere mist
quickly fading,
what we need is a constant river,
love of the people,
and a responsibility that flows
within the conscience.

teach our descendents with stories
that you have gathered from real memory
so that they may know themselves,
dive into the world within emotions,
or swim out to god's great world.

think with a heart of humanity all that has happened
and foretell the future shape of time
unfold in the lap of experience the design of history
so that knowledge that fears no kris
may rise from them.

write,
write with all the tools of the bard's trade
so that from the past may rise greatness,
from our history we may learn the truth.

(*translated by Muhammad Haji Salleh*)

Chapter Twelve

'. . . His Majesty did not know the Prime Minister was
coming, so the doors were closed. Prime Minister thought
"The Sultan is angry with me, that's why the doors are shut."
He was so humiliated; returning home, he drank poison and
died.'

i

life has its own reasons:
a world of happiness or an afterworld of eternity,
floated on a religion that comes
in verses and interpretations,
softened by the villages and cities,
a child's cry and female persuasions.

i know, god cares for us,
watching the end as he does the beginning,
arranging the road in-between.

but i am a small being
locked within the palace, human words
and my own senses.

i have a master,
each emotion must be buried
under his wrath or reason,
i arrange my words, each morning.
that they may climb
and curl his lips,

bloom into his eyes.
i have a master.

a master is the ambiguous friend-adversary,
here goodness is quickly
fermented by verbal honey,
or sold for a gift of gold from the ambitious hand.

ii

the door that shuts in my face
slams into my future,
its dark wood darkens the sun.

(*translated by Muhammad Haji Salleh*)

Chapter Thirty-Two (ii)

'During these times Melaka was full of people, all manner of merchants gathered here; markets lined the way from Air Lilih to Kuala Muar; and from Kampung Keling to Kuala Penajuh there was no longer any need to bring the fire, as whenever one stopped one found houses; from this side of the country to Batu Pahat, too, Melaka was full of people, because during these times the subjects of Melaka were one hundred and ninety thousand altogether.'

i

and in the season of fruits, flowers and mangoes
shower colours into the dark green of leaves
all along the road of villages.
fruit fragrance floats into fields and appetites
doors and noses of children fishing in streams,
into memories of ancient women and young maidens
pounding rice,
into the calculations of new merchants adding profits
for a harvest-time dowry.

the mangoes of air lilih are as sweet as muar's *rambutan*
the *durian* of durian daun are red as polished copper
the *kedondong* of jugra are brittle on teeth of girls waiting
for the wedding.
all along the way *jambus* fall into their shadows,
dukus turn purple on trees, tubers fill into the hill-sides.
in the night bananas are shared with birds and foxes,
sentuls rot between their branches, the *langsat* is wasted.

bullock carts nod into kampungs,
from air lilih wheels whine uphill
and loosely chase down wet and green valleys.
each time the bulls are tired or my son cries
a small village awaits behind the hills.
water and fire are offered with an invitation
to taste new fruits and rest on the verandah.
the gay goodbye is loaded with
baskets of *langsat* and parcels of *duku*.

ii

melaka's house is wide-lawned
        a sail-roof and verandah breezy
do stop by, good friend
        the sun is hot, the day yet early.

a sail-roof and verandah breezy,
        steps of stone and china tiles
the sun is hot, the day yet early
        the morning has come to our stalls.

steps of stone and china tiles
    carved windows with swinging doors
the morning has come to our stalls
    with terengganu *songket* and hued head-dresses

carved windows with swinging doors
    dandies from kedah's realm
with terengganu *songket* and hued head-dresses
    you may test these blades from mataram

dandies from kedah's realm
    bajus are sewn by tailors of palembang
please try these blades from mataram
    handsome on the young, defenders of kampungs,

bajus are sewn by tailors of palembang
    worn by courtiers from upstream
handsome on the young, defenders of kampungs
    the style malay and the craft a dream.

iii

the smell of the market hypnotises five villages from *pandan*
                         mats and platforms
rafting upstream, calling to remote collectors
    to gather their rattan, rubbers and mountain roots.

makcik embun sells *dodol* that glitters like sumatranese gold,
its shine is filmed with oil of the *gading* coconut.
a tray of sweetmeats from grandmother jam's kitchen,
its rice clear, its sugar melaka.
maksu melur, the wife of pak lela,
the puppeteer of sungai rambai,
carries on her head cakes of many tastes
to the market, to which she comes late,
because her cakes are many, and so are her children.

at the southern end of the market *abang* nadim sat before his
                                  cencaluk,
his vase clean, his *baju* the colour of the bay,
his shrimps, fine, taken from tanjung kling,

when the water was calm and the moon full.
the heap of fishes is offered with pride.
senangis for friers or kedah curry,
terubuk for afternoon roasts,
then there are the ray fish and mackerel for the whole family,
sauteed shrimps or squid with vegetables,
peppered mussels, shells in coconut and lemon grass
and the most delicious, *ikan parang* for *masak asam*.
all the fishes are arranged on the scaly board,
pulled up by his nets from the dawn straits.

iv

the melakans are numerous and the streets loud,
all day long the market is coloured with people
clothes splashed to the trees and bushes
and the dark of the shadows.
at the junction a *minangkabau* man dramatises his medicines
cures for rheumatism, failing eyes or desires,
for old muscles and receeding energies.

at the edge of the village a young man plucks his *kecapi*,
accompanying the sad song of a broken-hearted singer.
from between the knotted sounds of the bazaar
the drums beat out a *dondang sayang*,
tempting feet to remembered steps,
to dream of dances with the kampung beauty,
returning old men to a rhythmic youth,
to old stories, stowed away from children.

traders come, all morning from surrounding hamlets,
from northern towns and creeks that drain brown hills,
bringing honey from forest trees, coconut sugar,
cloths from a thousand malay islands,
all taken from the earth, sea and air.

malacca is prosperous because it is proud,
big because its knowledge of life is from a weighing mind,
unafraid of the new, and always aware of the wrongs.
there were a hundred and ninety thousand then,
when the country believed in its people.

(*translated by Muhammad Haji Salleh*)

The Teller of Tales

this is a small and straight tale
that i have not picked from history's fragments
or lifted from the sketch on its backdrop.

this fine universe
is like the mushroom that sprouts
from the freedom and darkness of emotions
and a raindrop dilates into a universe.

what i may add
are mere brittle branches of anxiety
shoots and blossoms of words
– this is the story's tree
wrapped over with meaning.

(*translated by Muhammad Haji Salleh*)

Sailor

Cast into the damp air by the waves he dreams
of embraces and language of women
welcoming him with deference
eventually gentled by air and water.
storm unwind at the door,
waves hiss at the beach's gradient,
his dreams are as green as ground.

bound to an iron bed
without the wave's boost and the empty skies,
all that he knows is only women's deceit,
who make love with their hands
in his pockets
and the quarrel with himself
that split his argument.

he returns again
to the world of his mind
to the calm seas before dusk
the gentle perfect mist.
all are in place
all bestowing a peace.

(*translated by Muhammad Haji Salleh*)

Rahman Shaari

Rahman Shaari was born in Perlis on 5 September 1949.
He received his early education in Kangar and Kuala
Lumpur. Rahman received his training as a teacher at the
Sultan Idris Training College, Tanjung Malim in 1971.
He obtained his BA and M.Litt. from the National
University of Malaysia. Rahman Shaari writes creative
works – poetry, short stories and novels. His poetry has
several times received the highest acknowledgment, the
Malaysian Literary Prize. Rahman participated in the
International Writing Programme at Iowa University,
USA in 1991. He is currently a lecturer in the Faculty of
Education, University of Malaya. His collections of
poetry are: *Hamparan Kuning*, *Kesan Kunjungan*, and
Serpihan Diri.

In Turn

a pipe
the centre of a dozen houses
the water that pours from it
of greater repute than the sturdy body
of the man who stands and waits his turn

no shyness among those who wait
a man with a short towel
hurriedly shoves his empty bucket
beneath the pipe,
he races with women in *sarongs*
who arouse no desire
they're bored from waiting.

ma'am don't flare up
we must wait a while
for we arrived here late
i, and the two ladies

there's no one more important accursed land,
give thanks for the pipe
that pours out water,
though we are forced to look sour
and wait our turn.

(translated by Barclay M. Newman)

Yellow Carpet

Returning home, now and then
I wish to seep the whole of you
into my innermost self
then to live with the flow of my blood
my folks' stream
of sincere love
who brought me up to free me
because they believe in knowledge

'the earth of this village', father said
'will not be as fertile
as that which spreads
in your breast'.

on the verandah
my eyes are bathed in the ocean of padi
a yellow carpet
you have flowed through my culture
a bosom friend who has once parted
returning to knock on the door of my conscience

I have now returned to you
with the old undying love
I return with old emotions
and a new mind.

(translated by Muhammad Haji Salleh)

The Old Woman and Her Dog

The old woman
takes her dog along
wherever she goes.

She's the estranged mother
of her children
whom she used to take along
wherever she went.

She commands and advises
the leashed dog
its understanding is of no importance
she must speak
to resist silence
there are no grandchildren by her
like my own grandmother.

Forgive me for asking,
dear old lady,
have you transferred
your house, land and property
to your dog,
as you are no longer visited by your children
and unknown to your grandchildren?

(translated by Muhammad Haji Salleh)

Drought

the day is made restless by your eyes
oppressing me in my warm room
body naked
and a mind enumerating failures
out there is mere heat
and flying dust.

this is time for thought
of the meaning and price of water.

(*translated by Muhammad Haji Salleh*)

Let It Be

I reduce my words
after much appraisal
this silence is precious.

What are words
if questions are answered
with new questions.

We have been long together
living and edging into tomorrow
warm breath in the night's coolness
or fatigue
in a time that should bring calm.

Life's values
perch over tomorrow
to reduce words
that consideration
is increased.

(*translated by Muhammad Haji Salleh*)

Outside the Group

if you turn from this road
discovering happier routes
perhaps better than this life
joining the processions of the father
till convictions are displaced

I am not fully me
a part yet undiscovered
eyes smarting
ears and lips bored with their functions.

I search for myself outside the groups
where I am stronger though isolated
here truth refers to the self
each arrogant breast will concur

(*translated by Muhammad Haji Salleh*)

SITI ZAINON ISMAIL

Siti Zainon was born in Kuala Lumpur on 18 December 1949. She received her early education at Kuala Lumpur before proceeding to Sekolah Tinggi Seni Rupa (ASRI), Yogyakarta, Indonesia (1970–73), where she graduated with a bachelor's degree in Fine Arts. She is currently a lecturer at the National University of Malaysia while completing her PhD dissertation at the University of Malaya. Several of her poems have won the Malaysian Literary Prize. Her poems are compiled in various anthologies of poetry – they are: *Nyanyian Malam* (1976), *Puisi Puteh Seorang Kekasih* (1984), *Perkasihan Subuh* (1986), and *Daun-daun Muda* (1986). A committed artist, Siti Zainon has written several articles and books on Malay art and culture. She was awarded the SEA Write Award in Bangkok in 1989. An English anthology of her verse, *The Moon is a Candle*, appeared in 1992.

Platform

no more smiles, leaves are falling
autumn is almost here.
no more talk, there are still many tales to tell
but the storyteller has his coffee
the lamps have been extinguished
night grows dark, I close
my eyes, wrapped in dancing candlelight, I
allow time to run free, to remember, to meet
with my man, forgive me . . . your woman
is not as innocent as she should be.

(*translated by Harry Aveling*)

In the Curve of the Taj

I will cradle the moon, you said,
in the palm of my soul. The spring wind
blows across the earth. We lift
    the dark blanket of mist from the Taj.
They whisper. The birds, they say,
have sung their songs. The tops
    of the pine trees
will never grow tall. There will be no end
to the curve of the dome.

Your shadow
pierces
the marble. Before the dark moon fades
it tells me that God and I are one
touching the passing light
feeling strange miracles
on the lips of the night. A shifting face
passes
shining across the lake.

Ages are gone.
My prayer-beads bring you close
in time of prayer. In this memorial
I wonder if the fresh winds of love
still shake eternity. The blood rushed
    to my face
skips across the ripples of the Yumna
and burns in my soul!

Pray to the Greatest Lover of all
as the fingers of the wind brush
    the red sand
from the stones in the courtyard
shifts from the slender arrow of the moon.
For a while Hope and Truth
both flower.

(*translated by Harry Aveling*)

Siti Melorinda

You have planted this garden
     with green bushes
      and in between them my small flower
    sprinkled with the fragrance of the *selasih*.
into my woman's conscious
comes flying and perching
from Him
the rustling voice alights
a white song
on a clear night and rising moon
I welcome life's hues

my flower,
here
     a light velvet
the voices of thrushes and insects
in the wind-swept rain
its shudder mercurises nature
all His gifts
reflected in the blessing's mirror
     purple or grey
     anytime engulfing your fragrance

She is the most present
perfecting us, love
a garland of pearly hues
that becomes light
muffling the journey's dust.
     a voice from far heaven
    danced in the night
ending the restless dark
meaning from its search.
This is your Gift
that garlands my days.

(*translated by Muhammad Haji Salleh*)

Rainbow

The rain is falling
  on the hills
The ferns are open
  at the foot
  of the stairs

Come into my house
  the candles
  are burning

(*translated by Harry Aveling*)

Mogul Night Flute-Music

A song falls to his lips
    A tune created by a cord of breath
      Sorrow plucked from the gaps
        of our lives.

As the moon waits
Candles stand like nails
He picks the whispering leaves
    of this final night
      Flute at the hidden window
        Glass moon at day's end.

Before the window closes
Before the moon shatters
Knife and fork tear at flesh
    hunger raw on the plate.

She sips
at the sad soup of sorrow
Glasses of wine are raised
The flute sighs
knowing that soon

a candle will melt
and harden on the table
of her room.

(*translated by Harry Aveling*)

4th December 1985

They flew to heaven
as though in a deep sleep.

Goats and oxen fell to the ground.
Vishnu was angry
and wept.

Their eyes
saw only blood.
Their milk
turned to pus.

Between the old huts
the painful sight
of weary people
remains.
Will the rain fall,
will it renew
their corn and wheat?

Perhaps the disaster
was deliberate –
an old punishment
for their sin
and wickedness.

Overseas, men throw dollars at them
Blind men, with no light in their eyes.

(*translated by Harry Aveling*)

The Flute Player

His sadness
fills our soup bowls
with ancient blood
the pain of artist
as it falls from the tip of his flute.

Friend,
you see the tears,
the fingers beating with love,
the endless songs:
a few rupees
drop at his feet.

A taut
quivering
thread.

He is a poet:
the veins of his song
run with sorrow.

(*translated by Harry Aveling*)

Prayer

With a silver bangle on his wrist,
he has scattered bread in the fields,
there, for seven seasons,
for the crows to fight over.
I snatch a lightning silver hair from his soul
my thoughts are fixed
there, wondering how he lives
In Prayer
teaching a world
which knows only endless hatred,
rage and fear.

He knocks on one door after another,
leaving his Beads and his Blessings
for those he leaves sadly behind
needing his prayers.

He is tired of walking.
wrapped in his long gown.
up hill, through the valleys

> 'I pray for those
> who are frightened of the dark
> and bored by the day.
>
> This is the Water of Love,
> drink it, dear children,
> I pray you will be well.
> God has created us His Love
> God has created His Grace
> A miracle, freely given to all.'

Crows perch on his hands
as he scatters his bread. I will try
to hide in his shadow.

(translated by Harry Aveling)

T. Alias Taib

T. Alias Taib was born on 20 February 1943 in Terengganu. He received his education at Kuala Terengganu. He has written many poems, although in the early stages he wrote short stories. He is currently a teacher at a school in Kuala Lumpur. His published collections of poems are: *Laut Tidak Biru di Seberang Takir*, *Pemburu Kota*, *Seberkas Kunci*, and *Opera*.

Prostitute 4

like a book
i read your muddy lips
there are intelligible movements
there are waves crashing
to the shores of your heart

like a book
i turn your torn pages
there are unspoken words
there are voices that have lost their sound
in the folds of your eyes

like a book
i often guess the meaning of your face
from the strips of plot
disarranged
full of riddles

like a book
i enter into characters
who float in your laughter
i try to comprehend the flashbacks
that are rolled in your tears

(translated by Muhammad Haji Salleh)

Rat Race
(a portrait of kuala lumpur)

some run over with the intestines spilled out
some rolled over to the rivers' edge
some hungry
some swallowing their own mothers
some satiated
some dying from satiation
some mending their severed tails
some climbing over their friends' heads
some with their heads climbed over
some screaming
some musing
some drunk over heaps of rice
some crazy over piles of rubbish
some returning to their lovers' arms
some losing their way home

millions of rats loitering
challenged by the whistle.

(*translated by Muhammad Haji Salleh*)

A Push Cart

a push cart
lonely, leans
licked by the sun

between
a lane
and the mosque's fence

everything
depends
on it

for
the rojak salad hawker.

(*translated by Muhammad Haji Salleh*)

My World

i keep my world in a trouser pocket
my world keeps all the boundaries of my life
i roll it out through the day's door
it suddenly changes
into an enormous stone marble

if it breaks
you can read the maps of a thousand selves

padi fields stretching out, valleys stretching out
rivers like blood stretching out
flow by the edge of restless hills

ancient jungles stretching out, a rendezvous
for all animals for all vegetation
stretching out too is the clear night
that is lost for so long
from my eyes
deep in the city in dry dust
and the harsh rolling winds
deep in the city life is squirming
strangled in the
wounded walls

if my marble is broken
i shall read the strewn fragments of the self

(*translated by Muhammad Haji Salleh*)

Apple

there's a big garden in a magnificent hotel in the middle of the city. night lets her hair down over the shoulders of the forbidden tree by the fountain. from the darkness, suddenly a leaf of a wind drifts by and disappears immediately through the tree's veins and pulse. it frees itself and kicks from within the trunk, branches, leaves, stalks and fruits. obviously the tree is very weak and eventually surrenders.

there's a voice, soft and seductive from the mouth of a snake, wound around a tree. the voice wanders and sighs at the wet earth, approaching adam's and eve's shoes, while they are seated at a stone bench. they eye the forbidden fruit with an unusual desire. on the fruit is hooked the snake's poison. on the poison are beads of clear desire glittering, shot by moonlight.

in a few moments, you can hear the fiery breath that contains the snake's poison boiling and threshing the bushes. the bushes sway, followed by a loud scream from behind the sky, waking the whole garden. trees too become wild. the sky unsheathes a sword, chases them and repeatedly stabs at the bodies.

(translated by Muhammad Haji Salleh)

Secret

a single flower
a single drip of nectar
a grasshopper born then
know not their secret
beetles from afar
have flown miles to enjoy
the single flower
the single drop of nectar

(translated by Muhammad Haji Salleh)

Drought

the sun sprinkles its powder
on to the padi field's tongue

the clouds roll on, restless
in its heart
the winds break

the winds yawn
in the mouth of a buffalo
the thunder is stranded

silence and drought smoke
between the brown leaves
it does not rain

a dune stretches
in the gray heart
of a peasant.

the sun sprinkles
over the throat of a village.

(*translated by Muhammad Haji Salleh*)

Keys

May verse be like a key
That opens a thousand doors
(Vicente Huidobro)

with a bunch of keys in my hand
i expose the thousand wounds
for so long encased
i let the thousand sponges of misery
floating in my chest all
gather before your very eyes
so you would understand:

what's prosperity amidst hunger
what's harmony amidst inflation
what's happiness amidst sadness

with a bunch of keys at my feet
i enter the maze of a thousand doors
filled with lamentation and expectation of desperation
one such tale of a labourer one evening
the drain he was sweeping
the dry leaves fragments of his life
bits and pieces of the future
prayers of friends thrown asunder

with a bunch of keys before my eyes
i see the thousand miracles
a thousand riddles and life's puzzles
completely complicated, completely intricate
like the expedition to mount kinabalu
sometimes there's a beginning, but no ending
sometimes there's an ending, but no beginning
sometimes there's no beginning and no ending

with a bunch of problems in my mind
i toss the keys far, far away from my sight.

(*translated by Muhammad Haji Salleh*)

USMAN AWANG

Born on 2 July 1929 in Kota Tinggi, Johore, Usman
Awang attended schools in Johore before joining the
Malayan Police Force (1946). After resigning from the
police force in 1951, he went to Singapore, started
working as a proofreader with *Melayu Raya*, then
became a reporter, and later joined the editorial staff of
Mingguan Melayu. Usman joined *Utusan Melayu* as an
editor of *Utusan Kanak-kanak* and later as editor of
Utusan Zaman and *Mastika*. In 1962 he worked with
Federal Publications Sdn Bhd, and in 1963 joined Dewan
Bahasa dan Pustaka on the editorial staff of *Dewan
Bahasa*, *Dewan Masyarakat*, *Dewan Sastera*, and *Dewan
Budaya*, and headed its Literary Division. He was
accorded the Literary Pioneer Award in 1976. In 1982 he
received the SEA Write Award. In 1983 he won the
National Literary Award (Anugerah Sastera Negara),
and was conferred honorary Doctor of Letters by the
University of Malaya. His works are: short stories – *Dua
Zaman* (1965) and *Degup Jantung* (1963); plays – *Dari
Bintang ke Bintang* (1965), *Serunai Malam* (1966), *Tamu
di Bukit Kenny* (1968), *Tirai Zaman* (1969), *Kaki Langit*
(1971), *Muzika Uda dan Dara* (1976), and *Drama-drama
Pilihan* (1987); novel – *Tulang-tulang Berserakan* (1966);
poems – *Gelombang* (1961), *Duri dan Api* (1966), and
Puisi-puisi Pilihan (1987).

Voice from the Grave

i

Mother
weep your old tears
from an older poverty
I see they offer wreaths
and lengthy condolences
most impressive
over our bloody death.

95

Father,
no more will you receive the few dollars
I wrung each month from a wretched pittance
(my pay: cost of one suit for a minister)
and my promise of a new roof for the hut –
forgive me, father – will never be fulfilled.

Dear wife,
your grief shall not last long
I hear they are collecting donations
why such kindness after we are dead
in life did they ever ask
about our crowded rooms, our month's pay.

Dear children,
your school uniforms are torn
you will have to patch them again
and who will buy your books this year?
Like your father
dream on, dream on my children
if you still possess dreams:
that you will study at the university.

ii

They talk a lot about my death
they grieve and get donations
but they could never spare a piece of land
no land ever for us
except for burial
(even this, one day they shall think
how much better to build a factory on it)
They who never noticed us
they who never asked about us
now write and deliver speeches
and call us national heroes.

Dear friends, you and I have died
for a prosperity not ours
so the owners may sleep and dream deep
so each estate can gather its rubber

so each mine can pile up its tin
so each bank can count its profits
so each industry can survey its products in peace
(for all this is not ours!)
for these we die.

Parliament meets with Royal speeches
Rural progress – Prosperity for the people
and schemes for raising taxes
by the brilliant Finance Minister.

Our death is talked of for a while
then with the gift of a cheque –
payment for my life, forgotten by all
except my mother, father, wife
and beloved children who shall suffer
all their lives.

(*translated by Adibah Amin*)

Black Snow

Leaves of pine
in the heat of the maroon moon
        advancing in line
upon the busy city
moving forward
like the trees into Macbeth's view
here the snow has another colour
        black
            black
                BLACK

this is
the mightiest colour
it does not fall from the stars
nor from the skies,
it flows from the currents of history
            BLACK

bones
fertilizing the rich fields
of prosperous America
black snow
      BLACK
deep black is the colour
      WE SHALL OVERCOME
in the south in the north
everywhere
caressing the historic wound of forefathers
today
    now
        most dazzling
        black snow.

(*translated by Muhammad Haji Salleh*)

Beloved

I'll twine the froth of the sea
    into a rope
    to tie you

I'll weave the waves
    into a carpet
    for your bedchamber

I'll spin the clouds
    into a veil
    for your hair

I'll sew the mountain winds
    into a nightgown
    for you

I'll pluck the star of the East
    a brooch to sparkle
    on your breast

I'll bring down the darkened moon
    a lamp to light
    my desire

I'll sink the sun
    embrace your seas of night
    drink your crystals of honey

My beloved how many dreams
    murder reality
    with illusions of heaven

(*translated by Adibah Amin*)

Under the Shadow of Red Tulips

Snow-fall has ceased
thinning whiteness
melts in dim daylight
    sink in black might
    of rock mountain
    swallowing steel chains
I smell the wounded day-air
acrid tear-gas in all cities, all campuses
flowers weep
    red tulips
    bloom bleeding
the day throbs with pain
from the wound of Vietnam's history
honour of kembodia
    M–i carbines scream their might in Kent State
four bodies lie stiff
shadowed by red tulips
as spring weeps

next day 60 pt bold-headline in Kent State papers:
AMERICA IS DEAD!
. . . it takes a blood bath

(*translated by Adibah Amin*)

Father Utih

I

He has one wife – whom he embraces until death
five children who want to eat every day
an old hut where an inherited tale is hanging
a piece of barren land to cultivate.

The skin of his hands is taut and calloused
accustomed to any amount of sweat
O Father Utih, the worthy peasant.

But malaria comes hunting them
even though he offers a million prayers
and Mother Utih calls the village medicine man
for magic formulas, curses repeatedly chanted.

The medicine man with his reward goes home
with money and a pullet tied together.

II

In towns the leaders keep shouting
of elections and the people's freedom,
of thousand-fold prosperity in a sovereign state
a golden bridge of prosperity into the world hereafter.

When victory brightly shines
the leaders in cars move forward, their chests thrust forward
ah, the beloved subjects wave their hands.

Everywhere there are banquets and festivities
delicious roast chicken is served
chicken from the village promises prosperity

Father Utih still waits in prayer
where are the leaders going in their limousines?

(translated by Adibah Amin)

Greetings to the Continent

I
They separate us
the passports visas frontiers all names for barriers
they rob us with their laws
sending bullets wrapped in dollars
forcing us to choose
and choose we must
there is no other way

II
Friend, you have chosen guns and bullets
many leaders prefer their dollars
for this you must soak your clothes
red glass, red river
children's weeping
the blood of the exploited

III
You squeeze cactus and grind stones
to make food and drink
girls toil decorated in dust
little children sling on their weapons
you darken the sky with exploding pipelines
others sing in prisons
for the freedom of Palestine

IV
We strive in drying rice-fields
strong peasants have begun to clear the virgin
                                                    jungle
small beginnings in a cloudlike calmness
a calmness that nips us in the bud
we the few are still learning
from all your experiences,
and you own
we shall consolidate the May eclipse
at the true target
at this archipelago

(*translated by Adibah Amin*)

The Times

This is a time of bitterness,
The stench of blood fills the air,
All voices are buried in silent chests.

Beware when you speak to anyone,
Eyes penetrate from between prison cells.

You, the poet, will write all,
Your sharp pen can cut into all suffering!
The times teach you to live in hypocrisy
Or save your skin with nods.

You, the journalist, gather the news of mankind,
Your sharp pen can dig into their follies!
You are silent, hand clapsed under the table,
The times force you to write only of the good.

Everything oppresses, because over them is forged iron,
Everything bores, because they are all false.

(translated by Muhammad Haji Salleh)

Letter from the Bird Community to the Mayor

Lord Mayor
we the bird community called a meeting
one fine clear morning
on the roof of the deserted Parliament building.

All sent their intellectuals to represent them,
all but the crows, for they were too busy
mourning their loved ones, shot dead
and drifting down the River Klang.

Special guests came as observers,
a delegation of butterflies,
involved in the issue.

Lord Mayor,
though we had no hand in electing you
since franchise is not for the feathered,
still we honoured you for your promise
OF A GREEN CITY.

Alas, they have desecrated THE GREEN of nature
to worship THE GREEN of dollars
since Kuala Lumpur's mud turned to concrete
we birds have been the silent sufferers
the late *Belatuk*[1] was crushed under a felled tree
Merbuk[2] was conned by the name Padang Merbuk
while he and his kind were cooped in cages.

The *Pipit*[3] delegation are protesting
against the insult in your proverb
'pipit pekak makan berhujan'
(deaf sparrows feed in the rain)
Pipit and *Punai*[4] both feel
it's most improper of you to call
certain private parts of your anatomy
by their names, when you well know
your 'pipit' and 'punai' can't fly
(you have deflated our egos
in the process of erecting yours).

Lord Mayor,
this letter requests that in your wisdom
you will protect each branch, each root,
each leaf, each petal, each bower,
for these have been our homes through the centuries,
and it would also be for the good of man,
his health and happiness, his peace of mind,
to let nature and its myriad beauties bloom
in the brilliant sun.

[1] wood pecker
[2] turtle dove
[3] sparrow
[4] wood pigeon

(*translated by Adibah Amin*)

Little Girl

Her body reminded me of
areca palm in quiet country
tall and thin
in heavy storms
broken branches fall around
but the palm stands erect
awaiting the morning sun.

So it was with this little girl
thin as areca palm
year after year meeting her father
across the barbed wire of a prison
imprisoned these many years
courageously fighting oppression
steady and faithful.

This little girl surprised me
calm and smiling broadly
politely turning down my help
'I don't need money, uncle,
just paper and books.'

Young in age
her soul matured by experience
not everyone grows strong this way
a unique steadiness that charms.

When I expressed sympathy and sadness,
feeling sorry for her,
once again she smiled and said:
'Don't be sad, uncle, steady your heart,
there are many children like me in the world.'

I became quite still
she calmed me, this little girl
pacifying waves of emotion
forbidding pity for her bitter experiences.
Is it not shameful for a grown man,
wanting to help suffering prisoners

to receive counsel from the child of one in prison
to be brave and steady?

Ten children like this
will destroy the purpose of a thousand prisons.

(*translated by Adibah Amin*)

Can Mother Crab Teach Her Young to Walk Straight?

In truth, Mother Crab has never attempted to teach her young
to walk straight since she is pretty well convinced that what
Mother Nature has decreed for generations of crabs should not
be tampered with. In other words, the peculiar gait of the crabs
is both correct and beautiful. On the other hand, the crab
community look upon human beings with some incredulity, as
their life always seems to be hamstrung by endless doctrines
and edicts, circulars and memoranda, parliamentary acts and
high faluting principles, all of their own making. Human
beings spend a considerable amount of their lives formulating
all kinds of rules and regulations and supervising their
implementation. There are traffic rules, dress rules and
punch-card rules; there are rules on parliamentary debates;
there are the Court regulations, water regulations, electricity
regulations and even regulation against long hair (for those
well-endowed). Mother Crab is in even greater wonderment to
see human beings waste so much of their time in self-
beautification applying facial makeup, hair shampoo and in
dressing up. Not a few of them are over-conscious of trimming
their weight down to the extent of starving themselves
subsisting only on capsules and 'jamu-makjun' both for
sustenance or for strengthening certain vital organs. Others go
on about ties, their ancestry, their social status and official
designations. Yet others are so obsessed with shaving their
facial hair clean in between fighting and killing each other, or
oppressing and cheating one another. Having said all that,
should we not ask ourselves then – who really should teach its
young to walk straight, Mother Crab or Man?

(*translated by Adibah Amin*)

WAN A. RAFAR

Wan A. Rafar was born on 3 February 1947 in Kelantan.
Having completed his secondary education, he studied at
the Language Institute, Kuala Lumpur. He obtained his
BA (Literature) from the University of Malaya in 1974.
Wan A. Rafar writes poetry and literary essays. His
poems have won the Malaysian Literary Prize for the
years 1971, 1974 and 1982. He is currently teaching in
Sekolah Menengah Kuala Kerai, Kelantan.

Bagong

i'm bagong
bagong seri alas
descended from a mountain of brass
a fertilized creature
i'm bagong
a drop of blood from a god
protected by gods
i'm bagong
walk without feet
fly without daggers
i'm bagong
walk a little, run a lot
step forward and don't come back
i'm bagong
i turn jungles into fields
and night i turn to day
i'm bagong
once i shouted 'hah!'
time stopped and roads became lonely
i'm bagong
a hunter of the future
which leaps from dreams

and springs from shadows
i'm bagong
don't meet the edge and end
who hinders? who troubles?
i'm bagong
snap the neck and tear the body
i'm bagong
live in blood, live in fire
i'm bagong
fill a female
with my seed
i'm bagong
guardian of heaven and earth
i obstruct the rain
wow, i'm bagong
remember!
i'm bagong
who's bagong
who am i?

(*translated by Muhammad Haji Salleh*)

A Couple of Bodies

I am your subject
smaller than the ant
and you are my country
a body stretched out
from the asian mainland.

I would like to travel
along the capes and curves of your body
from the johor of your toes
to the perlis of your hair's end
or from the left side to the right side.

I would like to wrap myself
around your not-too-slender waist

padi fields and rubber estates
to cross rivers that often
carry the hinterland's grief
fresh hills and valleys
the ever expanding cities
the thick jungles and the long beaches
highways that challenge travel
all these would I venture.

I would like to dive
into the bed of your soul, free from anxiety
I would like to feel
the path of your thoughts and the mind's ways
the web of your pulse and blood
I would like to trace
your long and branching history
but I am your subject
smaller than an ant
that has just perched on your toes.

And forgive me, if I
am not your knight.

(*translated by Muhammad Haji Salleh*)

Stone

it did not dream
it did not desire
        to become a house

it kept still
        while being transported
        from the hill of its origins

it did not complain
        while its body was smashed
        to become gravel for the roads

when its blood flowed
it did not cry out in pain

it was too good for human beings.

(*translated by Muhammad Haji Salleh*)

Without You

without you
the clock does not tick
the rain does not fall

without you
the birds do not fly
the fish do not swim

without you
the lips lose their speech

without you
sleeps loses its dreams
space loses its silence

without you
you lose me
I lose you.

(*translated by Muhammad Haji Salleh*)

ZAIHASRA

Zaihasra, whose real name is Zaiton Abdullah, was born on 28 February 1951 at Alor Gajah, Melaka. She received her secondary education in Melaka. Several of her poems have won the Malaysian Literary Prize. Her collections of poems are: *Balada Tun Fatimah, Dalam Pelarian I, Dalam Pelarian Tiga, Aquarium Kota,* and *Laut, Pohon dan Kota.* Zaihasra worked with Radio Television Malaysia from 1974–81. Before she died on 22 November 1989 of a kidney ailment, Zaihasra had been active in commercial landscaping and directing film documentaries.

The Ocean at Dawn

The ocean at dawn,
is neither rousing nor silent

the ocean at dawn
is neither cruel nor terrifying

the ocean at dawn
is a maiden who has just tasted
life's joy on her wedding night
bliss inundates her body
ecstasy mingles with enchantment.

She wants to tell the world what has happened
but in the glow of the happiness that morning
she is bashful remembering
all that terrified her the first time
yet that is love – soft and shy.

the ocean at dawn
is a girl who relishes longing
with a secret modesty

the ocean at dawn
when the sky and the sea meet at the horizon
is a magic world
where ripples tease the swelling waves, and waves cheer!
the ocean at dawn
marks a new phase in time, the dawn of womanhood.

(*translated by Noor Aini Osman and Muhammad Haji Salleh*)

Here Time Wounds a Love that Fades

Late in life we discover
a world whose form
speaks
farther and farther
i leave behind the frozen past
here nerves of confidencce
explain its existence

and then i understand
that time which wounds
is not a hurt
for hurt is a sign of passion for life
which tortures with longing

time which wounds
instructs a woman's desire
colours the imagined eclipse of her sky
bloom forth the truth

that truth which causes me to dream
of green leaves before they fade
when breezes caress and promise gentleness
but never hint of typhoons
which change each vow
that's made

i understand more and more
(thanks for all you've taught)

here time which wounds
plants deep a sign of love that fades

(*translated by Barclay M. Newman*)

A Moment Put to the Test

at moments you create like this
the solitude's a test of separated love
it challenges the purity of womanly devotion
within the gentleness of a day so full of mystery

imagine seconds full of throbs
my hair is stroked by dim rays
my lips and your lips unite
to kiss me meaning of life that bleeds
and then, in purity like this
with sobs and a wife's modesty
separation comes and challenges promised trust
when faithfulness no longer hangs from my hair
and lines of love no longer show on your brow
but love is met in the glance that astounds
and in memory that permits

and if the sun still trails my step
I'll surely recall those footsteps in the sand which meet
discoveries full of secrets
in life that's full of wounds

today in the dim sunset
I recall once more the days gone by
and I'm ready for days ahead
but, before that
I feel my trust is put to the test

(*translated by Barclay M. Newman*)

My City

I pursue the final phrase from this journey,
my city, then to become sure in speaking it
with belief, you are my city
where I visited and found alienation
its day wearing the complexion of night
and everything is apart.

my city,
I shall no longer guide your gravel
but shall only guide my own heart
under the humid winds I spread out my face
to the wide world that is still open
and I see everything, everything
as a knight who has lost his battlefields
my city
in the greed of your waves
you stride into dispersion
and open up, open up yourself
my city.

(*translated by Muhammad Haji Salleh*)

ZURINAH HASSAN

Zurinah Hassan was born on 13 June 1949 at Alor Setar, Kedah. She received her secondary education at Alor Setar, graduating with a BA from the Science University of Malaysia, Penang. Her poetry and short stories have won the Malaysian Literary Prize several times. Her collection of poems *Keberangkatan* won the second Putra Poetry Contest. Her other published poetry books are *Sesayup Jalan* and *Di Sini Tiada Perhentian*. Zurinah is currently working as an Information Officer with the Ministry of Information Malaysia.

In An Aquarium

In an aquarium
there are fishes wishing to swim
free and far
there are fishes in anger
against the four walls that restrain
their journey
beating their bodies
and then recognizing
that these walls frame the water
that give them
an aquarium
In an aquarium
the beautiful lily
has transformed every blossom
but is unable
to root itself down.

A traveller arrives
to find so much life
then discovers his lost self
during the journey.

(translated by Muhammad Haji Salleh)

The Other Love Poem

a sailor is in love with the waves
and eventually like the waves
he becomes a hopeless lover.

a poet is in love with words
and eventually the net of words
traps him from meaning.

the sea is an infatuating spread
the jungle a passionate net
but the sea will not confess its secret
the jungle will not confess its secret
and the self becomes
a pinnacle of mystery.

all creation is a medium
to a recognition of the creator
yet how shall I write a poem of love
so that the medium
does not hide the purpose?

(translated by Muhammad Haji Salleh)

With the Earth's Dust

The longer the time, the further I am from home, mother
fresh breezes play with the curtains in the living room.

The drift of time threw me here
the lonely hunter. The neon lights attract me each night
and each second, in love the dust caresses my face

Here the minarets make us turn from one to another
mother has willingly surrendered me
to the earth's dust
struggling with the most faithful followers
we have become part of the machine.

Mother, in this space
earth's dust stifles love
yearning is pain most bitter
and we no longer know how to cry.

(*translated by Noor Aini Osman*)

Looking for Space

Suddenly he got up and switched off the light
saying, 'This room is bigger in the dark
since we cannot see the walls'.

I switched on the light again
saying, 'This light is the space
we are more often imprisoned
by the walls that we cannot see'.

(*translated by Zurinah Hassan*)

Marriage
(*one woman's opinion*)

Marriage
is the difficulty of giving up what you'd like to do
and feeling less yourself
and a woman
often becomes less herself
in order to be more a woman.

To a woman marriage
is a protection
for her who cannot afford the high price
and the high risk
of living with her own identity.

(*translated by Zurinah Hassan*)

Are You Still Playing Your Flute

Are you still playing your flute
when there is hardly time for our love
I am feeling guilty
to be longing for your song
the melody concealed in the slim hollow of the bamboo
uncovered by the breath of an artist
composed by his fingers
blown by the wind
to the depth of my heart.

Are you still playing your flute
in the village so quiet and deserted
amidst the sick rice field
while here it has become a luxury
to spend time watching the rain
gazing at the evening rays
collecting dew drops
or enjoying the fragrance of flowers.

Are you still playing your flute
the more it disturbs my conscience
to be thinking of you
in the hazard of you
my younger brothers unemployed and desperate
my people disunited by politics
my friends slaughtered mercilessly
this world is too old and bleeding.

Is this the end of our love
time is forcing us, as artists
to live outside ourselves.

(*translated by Zurinah Hassan*)

Certainty

you may not be the best man
but for a woman like me
perhaps there's no one better
than you.

i may not gain all
but in my condition
i request for
nothing more.

do not enquire whether i am happy
i too will not enquire of your emotions
for when one wants to be too certain
one becomes more doubtful
saying and analysing too much
one knows less.

perhaps i am less certain
of what i have spoken
but what is certain is that
we need not be too certain.

(translated by Muhammad Haji Salleh)

Waves at My Feet Waves in My Heart

you are to me
my sea
because i adore your voice
you are to me
my beach
because i understand your language
you are to me
o sweet whispers of the wind
the melancholic melody of the sea
background music
to my restless drama.

waves at my feet
waves in my heart
lashing
. . . the rocks
rolling
hugging
the poet at its side is caressed
with words as happy as the sand
   as loving as the wind
      as cordial as the waters.

how willing, the sand at my feet
how faithful the heart's throb
the froth's laughter becomes merrier
the dance of leaves becomes more passionate.

the chill of the beach is brought home
a single leaf in the hair
a panoramic glance in the eye
as lasting as the heat's feelings
   your song is willing
      my song is faithful
         an eternal flute.

(*translated by Noor Aini Osman*)

Life from a Train Window

life is a panorama from a train window
in the midst of a journey determined by rails
a panorama that glides past
an eternally changing scene.
the self, is it a great mountain
that is indifferent
to the winds that caress its breast
to the clouds that lovingly approach it
or is it no better than proud weeds
that firmly condemn

and thrive on hatred?
is it water descending
with violent force
an unbridled voice of anger
at the unsolved mystery of the jungle
falling at last to become foam?

i laugh at myself from between the rocks
like the river in its senility surrendering itself to open fields
loyally following its turnings
gloomy and heavy-hearted.
there are festivals of leaves everywhere
dancing to the rhythm of the wind
before high noon they have turned
before twilight sapless.
the sudden downpours
screen the windows from nature's carpets
they determine which person's footsteps
will always remain alien
meetings and partings
happen without warning.
i search for myself in all things that pass the window
streaked faces
that change their colours
before I can make out their shapes
the train pulls its alien coaches
toward another station.

(translated by Muhammad Haji Salleh)

Dewan Bahasa dan Pustaka

OTHER ENGLISH TITLES IN TRANSLATION

Salina (1991)
A. Samad Said
Translator: Hawa Abdullah

The Morning Post (1990)
A. Samad Said
Translator: Hawa Abdullah

Wheels Within Wheels (1992)
Arena Wati
Translator: Hawa Abdullah

Jungle of Hope (1990)
Keris Mas
Translator: Adibah Amin

Fables of Eve (1991)
S. Othman Kelantan, Anwar Ridhwan, Siti
Zainon Ismail, Khadijah Hashim, Shahnon
Ahmad, Fatimah Busu
Translator: Harry Aveling

After the War and Other Stories (1991)
Anwar Ridhwan
Translator: Adibah Amin

'Ayn – Poems of Faith (1992)
Kemala
Translator: Harry Aveling

History of Malay Literature Vol. I (1992)
Safian Hussain, Modh. Thani Ahmad, Johan
Jaaffar
Translator: Hawa Abdullah

History of Malay Literature Vol. II (1992)
Ahmad Kamal Abdullah, Hashim Awang, Ramli
Isin, Sahlan Mohd Saman, Zakaria Ariffin
Translator: Khidmat Terjemahan Nusantara

The Opera House (1992)
Zakaria Ariffin
Translator: Solehah Ishak

Children of This Land (1992)
Noordin Hassan
Translator: Solehah Ishak

Protest (Modern Malaysian Drama) (1992)
Dinsman, Hatta Azad Khan, Johan Jaaffar
Translator: Solehah Ishak

The Moon is a Candle (1992)
Siti Zainon Ismail
Translator: Harry Aveling

The Sakura Petals Unfold (1992)
Arena Wati
Translator: Mohd. Tajuddin Samsuddin

Seeds of Love (1992)
Azizi Haji Abdullah
Translator: Harry Aveling

All the above titles are available from Dewan Bahasa dan Pustaka,
PO Box 10803, 50926 Kuala Lumpur, Malaysia.

In Print

NEW AND FORTHCOMING BOOKS

Traveller's Literary Companion to South-east Asia *by authors based in South-east Asia and the School of Oriental and African Studies, London.* South-east Asia has an important and relatively unknown literary history. The purpose of this book, as with all others in the 'Traveller's Literary Companion' series, is to make this literature accessible, both by copious use of extracts and by relating the literature to physical sites in South-east Asia. Both ancient and modern texts are covered and the volume ranges from the ancient texts inscribed on the walls of Thai temples to the vibrant modern literatures of Malaysia, the Philippines and Hong Kong. Western writers such as Maugham, Conrad and Graham Greene are also fully represented in this major literary guide. Countries covered include: Malaysia, Singapore, Indonesia, the Philippines, Hong Kong, Burma, Thailand, Laos, Vietnam and Cambodia. Includes black and white illustrations. *ISBN 1 873047 20 7 (hb), 1 873047 25 8 (sb), 432 pp (approx), hb £34.95 (approx), sb £12.95 (approx).* **Publication 1993.**

Traveller's Literary Companion series
Africa, Oona Strathern (forthcoming 1993)
Eastern Europe, James Naughton, ed (forthcoming 1993)
Indian Subcontinent, Simon Weightman, ed (forthcoming 1993)
True Tales of British India, Michael Wise, ed (forthcoming 1992)
Japan, Harry Guest (forthcoming 1993)
South and Central America, Jason Wilson (forthcoming 1993)
South-east Asia (forthcoming 1993)

Books on Japan
Alone in this World, Yoshio Markino
A British Artist in Meiji Japan, Sir Alfred East
Companion to Japanese Britain and Ireland, Bowen Pearse
A Japanese Artist in London, Yoshio Markino
Teaching English in Japan, Jerry O'Sullivan
The Tower of London, Natsume Soseki

All the above titles are available from In Print Publishing Ltd, 9 Beaufort Terrace, Brighton, UK. Tel: +44 (0)273 682 836. Fax: +44 (0)273 620 958.